I0146077

# Working to End Gender-Based Violence in the Disability Community

## Praise for this book

'In this impressive book, Tammy Bernasky amplifies the pivotal work of women and trans people with disabilities engaged in social movement mobilisation to bring an end to gender-based violence within the disability community. The book tackles a series of critical questions about the conditions and ethical orientations that shape advocates' repertoires of organising across nine different country contexts. An outstanding contribution to the field. A handbook for activists, advocates and scholars seeking to interrupt the normalisation of gender-based violence within the disability community.'

*Professor Karen Soldatić, Western Sydney University*

'*Working to End Gender-Based Violence in the Disability Community* makes significant contributions to social movement theory, as one of very few to address the gaps in gender and disability analysis in this field of social research. The book is based on Dr. Bernasky's qualitative inquiry with women and trans people working in disabled people's organizations in Australia, Bangladesh, Canada, Ghana, India, Kenya, and Nepal, the US, and Yemen.

The book is informed by Dr. Bernasky's expertise in qualitative and emancipatory research methods; institutional analysis; critical legal and policy studies; histories of critical social theory; and cutting-edge theorizations of structural violence, social transformation, and critical consciousness. The volume contributes to movement-building, and to transnational scholarship on disability and gender.

Dr. Bernasky is a highly accomplished and skilled social researcher who is deeply connected to local and international advocates focusing on gender, disability, and economic rights in an array of national contexts. Dr. Bernasky's insights on international community development; supranational policy analysis; and gender and disability rights were formed through her years of experience working as part of transnational disability-rights focused research teams.

I am delighted to endorse Dr. Bernasky's book!'

*Professor Rachel da Silveira Gorman, Critical Disability Studies,*
*York University, Canada*

# Working to End Gender-Based Violence in the Disability Community

## International Perspectives

Tammy Bernasky

**Practical ACTION PUBLISHING**

Practical Action Publishing Ltd
25 Albert Street, Rugby,
Warwickshire, CV21 2SG, UK
www.practicalactionpublishing.com

© Tammy Bernasky, 2022
The moral right of the author to be identified as author of the work has
been asserted under sections 77 and 78 of the Copyright Design and
Patents Act 1988.

All rights reserved. No part of this publication may be reprinted or
reproduced or utilized in any form or by any electronic, mechanical, or
other means, now known or hereafter invented, including photocopying
and recording, or in any information storage or retrieval system, without the
written permission of the publishers.

Product or corporate names may be trademarks or registered trademarks, and
are used only for identification and explanation without intent to infringe.

A catalogue record for this book is available from the British Library.

A catalogue record for this book has been requested from the Library of Congress.

ISBN 978-1-78853-195-5 Paperback
ISBN 978-1-78853-196-2 Hardback
ISBN 978-1-78853-197-9 Electronic book

Citation: Bernasky, T., (2022) *Working to end gender-based violence in the
disability community*, Rugby, UK: Practical Action Publishing
<http://dx.doi.org/10.3362/9781788531979>.

Since 1974, Practical Action Publishing has published and disseminated
books and information in support of international development work
throughout the world. Practical Action Publishing is a trading name of
Practical Action Publishing Ltd (Company Reg. No. 1159018), the wholly
owned publishing company of Practical Action. Practical Action Publishing
trades only in support of its parent charity objectives and any profits are
covenanted back to Practical Action (Charity Reg. No. 247257, Group VAT
Registration No. 880 9924 76).

The views and opinions in this publication are those of the author and do
not represent those of Practical Action Publishing Ltd or its parent charity
Practical Action.

Reasonable efforts have been made to publish reliable data and information,
but the authors and publisher cannot assume responsibility for the validity
of all materials or for the consequences of their use.

Cover design by Katarzyna Markowska, Practical Action Publishing
Typeset by vPrompt eServices, India

This book is dedicated to the folks who participated in my research and trusted me to tell their stories; and to the advocates and organizers who join them to work against gender-based violence in the disability community.

# Contents

# List of abbreviations

| | |
|---|---|
| ABA | Applied Behavioural Analysis |
| ADA | Americans with Disabilities Act |
| CEDAW | Convention on the Elimination of all forms of Discrimination against Women |
| CRPD | Convention on the Rights of Persons with Disabilities |
| DAWN | DisAbled Women's Network (Canada) |
| DPI | Disabled Peoples' International |
| DPO | Disabled People's Organizations |
| ILO | International Labour Organization |
| INWWD | International Network of Women with Disabilities |
| IYD | International Year of the Disabled |
| LGBTQI2S | Lesbian, Gay, Bisexual, Transgender, Queer and/or Questioning, Intersex, and Two-Spirit |
| NPR | National Public Radio |
| ODSP | Ontario Disability Support Program |
| PTSD | Post-traumatic stress disorder |
| RCMP | Royal Canadian Mounted Police |
| UNCRPD | United Nations Convention on the Rights of Persons with Disabilities |
| WHO | World Health Organization |

# List of figures

# Acknowledgements

This book is based on the doctoral research I completed for my Ph.D in Critical Disability Studies at York University in 2020. I would like to thank my doctoral supervisor Dr. Rachel da Silveira Gorman, and my committee members, Dr. Marcia Rioux and Dr. annie bunting. My dissertation committee was truly my dream team.

Dr. Rachel da Silveira Gorman's support and dedication kept me motivated as I carried out my research. Rachel's ability to support my work in a positive and meaningful way when I needed it, their constant encouragement, and the potential they saw in my work from the very beginning was invaluable. They made me feel enthusiastic about my work and the future time and time again. They are the kind of mentor and teacher I would like to be.

Dr. Marcia Rioux always guided me to be intentional in what I say and do. She encouraged me to think critically about what I read and write and to always think about what's not being said. Again, Marcia saw potential in me and my work before I knew it was there, and her ability to foster that kept me going through some difficult times. I am forever grateful for having known and worked with Marcia. She will be greatly missed by many.

Dr. annie bunting showed incredible sincerity, kindness, and encouragement in guiding me in my work. She brought a valuable perspective that helped me work through some important questions until I was satisfied with the answers.

Thank you to all of my family and friends for the continuous support and especially my parents for encouraging me to pursue my Ph.D and for insisting that I could indeed finish it. It was not a short journey, but it was an important one.

# CHAPTER 1
# Introduction

Violence and economic oppression affect women and trans people the world over, and women and trans people with disabilities face even greater risks than their counterparts. In Canada, for example, women with disabilities are more likely to live in poverty and on less total income than women without disabilities and men; they are less likely to be employed than women without disabilities and, when they are employed, they earn less (DAWN, 2019; Crawford, 2013; Malacrida, 2010). They are less likely to get married, more likely to get divorced (Muthukrishna et al., 2009), and are more likely to experience physical, sexual, emotional and psychological abuse (DAWN, 2013, 2019; Canadian Women's Foundation, 2014; Vecova Centre for Disability Services and Research, 2011; Brownridge, 2006; Olsvik, 2006). Lesbian, Gay, Bisexual, Transgender, Queer and/or Questioning, Intersex, and Two-Spirit (LGBTQI2S) people with disabilities face greater risks of violence, abuse and isolation than their counterparts (Lalonde et al., 2018; Bucik et al., 2017). Additional research on gender and disability oppression worldwide echoes these realities (Rodríguez-Roldán, 2020; Muthukrishna, et al., 2009; Braathen and Kvam, 2008; Mays, 2006; Cohen et al., 2005).

Women and trans people with disabilities are diverse. Our identities are made up of a number of characteristics and social locations which affect our life experiences. Women without citizenship status, Indigenous women, women of colour, poor women, and older women – like women and trans people with disabilities – share an increased risk of oppression. Oppression can happen based on any number of identity characteristics, but where these identities intersect is where the risk and form of oppression takes shape. Meanwhile, there are people within organizations who work against this oppression as community organizers and as self-advocates. Their motivations and experiences offer unique insight into the conditions that give rise to resistance movements.

To advance research on oppression from the vantage point of resistance movements, this book explores the motivations of advocates and activists who work against gender-based violence in the disability community. This is important, not only for understanding the impact of oppression on the self-perception of those affected by violence, but also in offering insight into what leads organizers within resistance movements to work against violence and other forms of oppression. This research provides a space for critical reflection and endeavours to support their continued efforts to improve the quality of life for people with disabilities experiencing gender-based violence and oppression. Collins says that,

> As people push against, step away from, and shift the terms of their participation in power relations, the shape of power relations changes for everyone. Like individual subjectivity, resistance strategies and power are always multiple and in constant states of change (2000: 275).

In this introductory chapter, I will identify key terms and their historical development. I will explain why research on resistance movements is important to me as a researcher and advocate, and why this work is critical for advancing efforts to end disability-based and gender-based violence.

I then position myself as a researcher and as a cis woman with a disability who has experienced some of the issues I have researched, thus finding myself in the simultaneous positions of insider and researcher. Research on resistance to disability oppression has, so far, largely excluded the specific challenges for women and trans people with disabilities who experience extensive forms of violence. I endeavour to begin to bridge this gap through interviewing community organizers and advocates who work on these important issues.

In Chapter 2, I establish my theoretical orientation to addressing gender-based violence in the disability community by centring the work of Paolo Freire, James Charlton, and Erving Goffman and drawing on feminist theory, critical race scholars, critical legal theory, and disability scholars in order to present a comprehensive understanding of oppression and empowerment. I trace the elements of a transformative process starting with the identification of oppressive material conditions and moving through to the conditions of an empowered consciousness. First, though, I address intersectionality and its critical importance to understanding experiences of oppression. Then I identify the everyday conditions of oppression and the factors that contribute to disability oppression. Here, I expand on the work of James Charlton in order to explore gender-based violence and disability. I give specific attention to consciousness among those working collectively to end gender-based violence. I end the chapter with an examination of the characteristics of an empowered consciousness and look at this in relation to social movement organizing. I give intentional attention to the unique circumstances of social movements led by women with disabilities.

In Chapter 3, I describe my recruitment methods, provide a profile of the participants who took part in the research, and share my method of analysis.

Chapters 4 and 5 focus on participant experiences as self-advocates and/or community organizers and the transformations they have experienced within themselves and in the movement over time. Chapter 4 focuses on participant experiences with representational issues, structural violence, rights issues, access to justice, and policy and government concerns. Chapter 5 focuses on the transformations, including the conditions that lead to these transformations such as access to education and seeing oneself reflected in the work, as well as the motivations identified by participants of wanting better for others, having a raised awareness, being supported within the movement, and seeing enhanced advocacy among women with disabilities. Each theme is introduced with a participant story which is highly reflective of that particular theme. I did this because it became increasingly important to me to tell participant stories as they were told to me. The totality of their experiences, in my mind, could not be separated into pieces. As a way to mitigate the risk of a lack of analysis across stories, I make intentional efforts to connect each participant's experiences to the applicable themes so that the commonalities are not lost to my organizational decisions.

In Chapter 6, I return to my theoretical framing. In this final chapter, I explore what my findings mean in light of what I have offered as my theoretical foundations in terms of oppression, consciousness, and empowerment in order to demonstrate the material conditions that come with moving through these processes. In doing so, I address the oppressive experiences described by the participants, the conditions that allow for a move to consciousness about disability oppression, and the subsequent or simultaneous empowerment of advocates and community organizers. I then offer the implications and further questions this research has raised for me before I conclude with a final reflection on the process of researching and writing about these issues.

## Definitions

Here, I want to draw attention to five terms used throughout this book that merit a discussion on meaning: disability, gender-based violence, intersectionality, oppression, and transformation.

To understand what is meant by **disability**, I defer to an internationally agreed-upon conceptualization. According to the United Nations Convention on the Rights of Persons with Disabilities, 'disability is an evolving concept and ... disability results from the interaction between persons with impairments and attitudinal and environmental barriers that hinders their full and effective participation in society on an equal basis with others' (United Nations, 2006: 1). Importantly, the way a participant identifies their experience during their interview is how it will be represented in this book.

I have chosen to use the term **gender-based violence** instead of violence against women because it carries with it an understanding of the power relations involved in experiences of violence based on gender identity. The European Institute for Gender Equality (2016) recognizes that 'Gender-based violence and violence against women are terms that are often used interchangeably as it has been widely acknowledged that most gender-based violence is inflicted on women and girls, by men.' However, use of the term 'gender-based' highlights two important points: that violence is committed against someone because of their gender identity or gender expression

(Status of Women Canada, 2018); and that many forms of violence against women are rooted in power imbalances and gender inequality (Peate, 2019; European Institute for Gender Equality, 2016). Specifically, it is violence that is the result of 'normative role expectations associated with each gender, along with the unequal power relationships between the two genders, within the context of a specific society' (Bloom, 2008: 14).

While the most common form of violence that women experience is intimate partner violence (Bloom, 2008), they are also subject to other types of violence including physical and sexual violence, sexual harassment, rape, trafficking, sexual exploitation, stalking, female genital mutilation, and foot binding (European Institute for Gender Equality, 2019; Deming, 2018). Women with disabilities experience a wider range of violence and they experience it more frequently than men with disabilities or women without disabilities (DAWN, 2019, 2013). They also experience specific types of violence that women without disabilities do not. For example, service providers may withhold assistive devices such as wheelchairs (DAWN, 2013), communicative devices, sign language, or medication (Cramer et al., 2004). Other types of violence include threatening to withhold services or devices, damaging devices, providing assistance in a violent manner such as rough transfers to wheelchairs, and violations of privacy (Odette, 2013).

Gender-based violence is multi-faceted and requires a multi-faceted approach. Deming (2018) argues that gender-based violence encompasses various types of violence and yet these experiences are not universal. The complexities of gender-based violence, then, require an understanding of violence as intersectional, further requiring an intersectional framework to understand the ways in which multiple factors influence experiences of violence and reactions to it. Morrison et al. (2007) argue that because risk and protective factors operate at multiple levels – relationship, community and society – corresponding interventions need to address all levels.

The Ontario Human Rights Commission (2014) offers a comprehensive definition of **gender identity** which reflects the complex nature of an individual's experience of gender:

> Gender identity is each person's internal and individual experience of gender. It is their sense of being a woman, a man, both, neither, or anywhere along the gender spectrum. A person's gender identity may be the same as or different from their birth-assigned sex. Gender identity is fundamentally different from a person's sexual orientation.

I offer this explanation because some of the participants in this research spoke about their gender identity, though not extensively, and how it relates to their experience doing advocacy or community organizing work. I frame my research as focused on gender-based violence in the disability community because, as my research progressed, it became evident that participants varied in their experience of gender and of disability. While I did not ask questions or focus on issues specifically related to trans people, I did ask participants to share their experiences more generally and, to the extent possible, I hope that I gave space to participants to disclose what they were comfortable with. It is, therefore, important to address what is meant by **trans** or **transgender.** Again, I turn to the Ontario Human Rights Commission (2014) for their explanation.

> Trans or transgender is an umbrella term referring to people with diverse gender identities and expressions that differ from stereotypical gender norms. It includes but is not limited to people who identify as transgender, trans woman (male-to-female), trans man (female-to-male), transsexual, cross-dresser, gender non-conforming, gender variant or gender queer.

**Intersectionality** is an important concept as it relates to identity and discrimination because discrimination is often impacted by intersectional identities. The term 'intersectionality' was coined by Kimberlé Crenshaw as part of her analysis of the Black woman's experience. She says, 'Because the intersectional experience is greater than the sum of racism and sexism, any analysis that does not take intersectionality into account cannot sufficiently address the particular manner in which Black women are subordinated' (Crenshaw, 1989: 140).

The Ontario Human Rights Commission, in its 2016 policy on ableism and discrimination based on disability, acknowledges that 'The concept of intersectional discrimination recognizes that people's lives involve multiple interrelated identities, and that marginalization and exclusion based on Code grounds may exist because of how these identities intersect'. Furthermore, the Commission takes an intersectional approach to discrimination, recognizing that multiple grounds often underlie human rights claims. They say:

> The concept of 'intersectionality' has been defined as 'intersectional oppression [that] arises out of the combination of various oppressions which, together, produce something unique and distinct from any one form of discrimination standing alone ...' An intersectional approach takes into account the historical, social and political context and recognizes the unique experience of the individual based on the intersection of all relevant grounds. This approach allows the particular experience of discrimination, based on the confluence of grounds involved, to be acknowledged and remedied. (Ontario Human Rights Commission, 2001: 3)

The fourth concept I wish to highlight is **oppression**. Iris Marion Young explores the manifestations of oppression in *The Five Faces of Oppression*. Young was a political feminist scholar interested in social justice and the politics of social groups. I draw on Young's work due to her ability to navigate and name the complex manifestations and implementations of oppression. She identifies oppression as structural and 'embedded in unquestioned norms, habits, and symbols, in the assumptions underlying institutional rules and the collective consequences of following those rules' (Young, 1990: 39). For Young, oppression is manifest in the

> deep injustices some groups suffer as a consequence of often unconscious assumptions and reactions of well-meaning people in ordinary inter-actions, media and cultural stereotypes, and structural features of bureaucratic hierarchies and market mechanisms – in short, the normal processes of everyday life (1990: 39).

Young sees oppression as enacted upon groups of people. Her understanding of *how* oppression is enacted makes room to explore oppression from an inter-sectionality perspective. Her work does not limit an individual to one specific group, nor does it limit the manifestations of oppression to a single output. Specifically, she identifies five manifestations of oppression: exploitation, marginalization, powerlessness, cultural imperialism, and violence. These will be explored in the next chapter. Consequently, oppression can affect different people in different ways based upon the composition of their identity.

Young states that these 'faces' of oppression appear in different combina-tions for different groups, and even for different members of the same group, based on their individual circumstances. Women and trans people with disabilities are no exception in their complexities and face any and all of these manifestations throughout their lifetime.

Finally, **transformation** in my work refers to a changed consciousness. Let me be more specific. Instead of accepting the conditions of their lives, the oppressed must first change their own attitudes about themselves (Morris, 1991). Freire (1970) theorized that to work against oppression there must be an object/subject transition. Consciousness-raising was central to his thesis: when individuals analyse their own reality, they become aware of their prior, distorted, perceptions and are able to develop a new, more accurate, perception of their reality. At this point they no longer accept negative biases and attitudes about themselves. The oppressed recognize their common experiences as oppressed people (Charlton, 1998), and once they perceive of their situation as oppressive, they seek to change it (Freire, 1970). Put simply, a changed consciousness encourages individuals to change the conditions in their lives (Collins, 2000). The oppressed then move from objects to subjects of transformation in their own lives.

## Situating myself in this work

I cannot separate myself from this project or my pursuit of disability rights and anti-violence work. I have, therefore, made a carefully considered decision to share some of my experiences as a way to state my subjectivity and my positionality within this work. This is my story.

I was about seven years old the first time I saw an adult with a physical disability like mine. It was then that I realized I was not going to 'grow out of it'. I remember feeling surprised and disappointed, not because it was difficult to walk (which it was), but because I didn't want to be different. I believed I was going to be like my parents when I grew up. I didn't have a community of people with disabilities to which I belonged or related, so I had no frame of reference to think about my disability or to understand it as a permanent part of me except in a medical setting, let alone to think positively about it. My family was always supportive. It never occurred to me that I could not do something until I actually couldn't do it. However, no one in my family had a my type of disability, and I did not see myself represented in media – or anywhere else, for that matter.

Upon entering school, my disability became a source of unwanted attention. Children would stare and say, 'What's wrong with you?' or, 'Why do you walk like that?' As I aged, I tried to hide my disability as much as possible. I never used the word disability to describe myself. My understanding of disability was informed only by the accessible parking space wheelchair symbol. I did not use a wheelchair and so I could not possibly *be* a person with a disability.

During my undergraduate degree I was once asked to speak about being a woman with a disability at a university event. I agreed but, as the day approached, I was too embarrassed. I told my professor I could not present but that I would still attend the event. At the last minute, when the professor announced that I could not be there, I stood and said, 'I'm here. I'll speak.' I don't remember much about what I said except that sometimes people assumed that I could not be smart because I have a disability. When I look back now, I feel that focusing on that aspect of my experience was not the best use of the platform I was given.

Around that time, I was also taking a human rights course and we were discussing the death of Tracy Latimer, a young girl with cerebral palsy who was murdered by her father. The man behind me, who was about the same age as my father, raised his hand and said that he would do the same thing as Robert Latimer if his daughter were like that. 'She wasn't really human, just a bunch of cells,' he said. I remember feeling afraid. I didn't speak. I remember thinking, though, that if my father thought like him, I'd be in trouble. I later went to see the professor because I could not let that incident pass without addressing it. At the next class I said, 'As a person with cerebral palsy, the comments that were made during the last class scared me. I'm glad that not everyone thinks like this man.' I said other things that I don't remember now. I think this was really the first time I had been forced to challenge perceptions of disabilities. I began to own my disability identity.

I travelled after university and encountered several situations where people would speak directly about my disability: God would bless me; I should pray more and I would be fixed; God loves me (even though I have a disability). I always challenged these ideas by telling people I did not want to be fixed. I eventually began working at an educational institute that focused on leadership development globally. The institute worked from an adult education perspective. My job was administrative in nature and I would often do physical tasks such as carry books, help set up classroom spaces, or give tours of our building. This tired me but it was the job I had accepted so I didn't try to change it at first. It was complicated. I developed an interest in disability issues because participants studying at the institute would ask me about disability issues in Canada.

My manager started sending me to conferences and events that were disability focused and I would return to the institute and give presentations. This really helped me begin to embrace my disability identity. I advocated for more disability inclusion in programme content but, as a member of support staff, I wasn't able to pursue it to the extent I would have liked. I did, at that time, start a community organization for people with disabilities so we could discuss issues in our small town and advocate for changes; one such effort being to successfully petition the town council for a safer accessible parking space near the local library.

A new branch of the institute where I worked was developed to focus on women's leadership. The manager of that programme saw potential in my abilities and encouraged me to apply for a position coordinating one of the programmes, which I did. She was not on the selection committee, which I note because transparency is important to me. I was hired and immediately began working well with my new manager. She gave me more programme development responsibilities and gave me space to include disability content in the programme. She even suggested that I use my health-care benefits to get a mobility scooter to use at work since our building was so big. I did just that because she said it in such a matter-of-fact way that I believed it to be a logical thing to do, and it was.

I became friends with a man whom I thought was interesting. We would occasionally spend time together and then, one day, he raped me. It changed me. Up to that point I was an optimistic person. I was known for smiling a lot. I was happy. When this happened, though, my world was no longer a safe place. The man harassed me for weeks. I had safety plans for work and home and lived in fear every day. Having been assaulted, I now understood that the risk of violence was always there. This was a difficult realization and exiting this situation was not easy. Being financially independent allowed me to access the resources I needed. I called a counselling support line and, traumatized as I was, I remember being impressed when the intake person asked if I needed access to a wheelchair-accessible counselling office. My disability became a part of my healing experience in some ways. During counselling we discussed how my disability influenced the way I was experiencing trauma. This was fascinating to me. I became aware that my disability and my gendered experience were connected, but I didn't fully understand how. My manager sensed that something was wrong and became very supportive. She recognized that I had taken my passion for disability as far as I could at my workplace and encouraged me to pursue a PhD in disability studies, perhaps starting with a master's degree to see if it was suitable for me. That is what I did.

During my master's degree I did not want to talk about gender or violence because it was too close to my own experience. At first, I wanted to forget what happened and focus on other things but, after making a short presentation for one of my classes on gaps in services for women with disabilities exiting violence, I knew that I was meant to pursue this full time. Bringing attention to the issues gave me a sense of purpose and the response I received from my classmates reassured me that I did the right thing in telling my story. I later applied to do a PhD and focus on violence and disability.

A month before I began my PhD in disability studies, I was again leaving an abusive relationship, an emotionally and psychologically abusive one, only this time I was financially dependent upon the man. Leaving was more difficult partly because of the financial stress and my housing insecurity. The experience caused me to broaden my understanding of violence to include socio-economic dependence. Studying for the PhD, issues that had directly affected me gave me a sense of purpose and hope. It continues to be a privilege to research issues I am passionate about.

This comes with responsibility. I must always be aware of my bias. I have a specific type of disability and a specific set of experiences. I have privileges as well as disadvantages. I have moved in and out of poverty, meaning my socio-economic status has fluctuated. I must always be aware that intersectional oppression is complex and further study is needed to understand its complexity. We may experience oppression in some aspects of our lives while simultaneously experiencing privilege in others.

The writing and research that came with pursuing my PhD changed my consciousness, based on what I now understand about consciousness. When I think of transformative education, this was the kind of learning I had imagined. I have come to understand the extent to which the structures in my daily life can work against me. For a long time, I took personal responsibility for the things I could not do. I see my life and the world differently now.

A particularly poignant example that comes to mind is reading Erving Goffman's book *Stigma*. I have thought a lot about people staring at me, probably because I experience it regularly – at times, daily. This affects a person. When I learned that someone wrote a book about this very thing, I felt as though I was not alone. I do not have a choice about when people stare at me. I would like to say that I have a choice in how I react to it but the truth is my reactions are often neither measured nor desired. Perhaps it is because I do not invite the curiosity of others. Nor do I invite their perceived entitlement to understand my movements in greater detail than what meets their eyes. I do often feel the burden of reacting in a socially acceptable way, though I am not afforded the same courtesy by those with the habits of staring and intrusive questioning. Sometimes I do not feel safe: for example, when people follow me, put their hands on me, or grab at me. Before pursing my PhD, I would be annoyed but I wouldn't think about how this type of harassment is a societal issue. I have become better at asserting myself, particularly when strangers ask me questions or say inappropriate things to me. Being a part of an academic programme where other people either identified as having a disability or identified as allies working towards equality and equity has given me more confidence to talk about disability and rights.

I could relate when participants in my project said that they do this work because they feel, 'How could I not do this work?' or because they do not want the same things to happen to others. This motivates me; and being part of a collective of people with the same priorities also sustains me. I am more aware now, and much more cautious about whom I let into my life and what I expect of them. Most importantly, I feel free. My motivation going forward is to create a better environment to support other women and trans people with disabilities experiencing abuse. I have seen increased commitment to these issues, and I want to be a part of those changes.

It is with my experience in mind that I have worked intentionally to limit the extent to which I map my life circumstances onto the things that I research and write about. I specifically want to know why other women and trans people with disabilities work on gender-based violence. When I learn about someone's work, I ask, 'What is your why?' Simon Sinek talks about inspirational leadership from a business perspective. He looks at what practices make some organizations successful while others are not as successful. He says, 'People don't buy what you do, they buy why you do it' (Sinek, 2009). While this applies to the business case, I believe it also applies to other work. When I think about organizations or work that has had a lasting impact on me, it is the stories of why people do what they do that have resonated with me. The work is important, and the motivation behind the work is often what initially gets our attention.

## Purpose

The chapters that follow explore consciousness about gender and disability oppression caused by violence, including economic dependency. I also look at the motivations of those working to resist violence and socio-economic oppression of women and trans people with disabilities. I draw on work that emphasizes consciousness and oppression; both the process of oppression and resistance to it. It will become clear that resisting oppression cannot be done without a raised consciousness. Freire (1970) and Young (1990) highlight the minimizing effects of oppression on a person's self-perception. I discuss this in the next chapter. For now, while I recognize the importance of studying the effects of oppression, I approach research on oppression from the vantage point of resistance movements in search of pivotal moments and motivations for activists and advocates to resist this oppression. Bannerji, in her work on gender and racial oppression, argues that non-white women need to produce knowledge in order to be reliable actors in history and that this 'knowledge cannot be produced in the context of ruling but only in conscious resistance to it' (Bannerji, 1995: 82). Similar sentiments apply to gender-based violence and disability oppression.

The project at hand places emphasis on giving voice to the experiences of those working on gender-based violence and disability. Traditionally, disability-related research treated the researcher as the expert and people with disabilities as the objects of research (Barnes, 1996). It was during the 1990s that researchers began to position people with disabilities as experts in their own lives (Kanter, 2011). This resulted in studies which document experiences of violence and barriers to accessing services for women with disabilities (Vecova Centre for Disability Services and Research, 2011; Malacrida, 2010; Braathen and Kvam, 2008; Cramer et al., 2004; Rioux et al, 1997).

An emancipatory research project on oppression of people with disabilities focuses on elements of reciprocity, gain, and empowerment (Oliver, 1997). It asks, 'What do the participants get out of the research?', 'Who gains from it?', and 'Can it be empowering?' Barnes adds that this type of research, '... must reinforce and help stimulate further the demand for change ...' (2003: 13). While emancipatory research may not be completely appropriate in Southern contexts (Singal, 2010; Stone and Priestley, 1996) and in Northern contexts where daily struggles for people with disabilities are for survival rather than emancipation, it can contribute to an ongoing process of empowerment.

There have been very few studies, if any, focused on the motivations and insights of self-advocates, organizers, and activists working on gender-based violence in the disability community. The DisAbled Women's Network (DAWN) Canada was the first feminist disability organization in Canada to address issues of violence against women with disabilities (Israel and Odette, 1993). They recently published a report that brings together existing research with additional research they conducted to establish a more intersectional lens in looking at violence against women and girls with disabilities. The report is aimed at providing a more holistic picture of the situation in Canada (DAWN, 2019).

As discussed in the next chapter, women and trans people with disabilities experience oppression like any marginalized group. Important to my work is understanding how oppression affects community organizers and advocates working to eliminate gender-based violence. Through my work, I seek to advance support of those working on these important issues.

# CHAPTER 2
# Theoretical framework

Women with disabilities experience violence and poverty in different ways and at higher rates than non-disabled women and all men. Similarly, trans women and transfeminine people experience heightened violence compared to transmen and transmasculine people (Slater and Liddiard, 2018). The Roeher Institute (1995) found that gender can affect the kinds of violence that occurs: for example, women with disabilities were more likely to experience sexual and emotional violence and abuse than men with disabilities. More recently, a United Nations Population Fund report on gender-based violence and disability found that people with disabilities are three times more likely to experience violence than those without; women with disabilities are ten times more likely to experience sexual violence; while 40–68 per cent of young women with disabilities and 16–30 per cent of young men with disabilities will experience sexual violence before the age of 18 (United Nations Population Fund, 2018a). One survey of trans and non-binary people found that 61 per cent of respondents with disabilities reported being sexually assaulted in their lifetime (National Resource Center on Domestic Violence, 2015).[1] LGBTQI2S women with disabilities and women of colour with disabilities are at greater risk of violence (Slater and Liddiard, 2018). There are advocates and activists worldwide working to end violence and socio-economic oppression of women, girls, and trans people with disabilities. Disabled women's organizations and community organizers operate in countries worldwide to eradicate violence and poverty.

The COVID-19[2] pandemic, which has required societies to isolate and reorganize, has not only illuminated many of the inequities to which people with disabilities have always been vulnerable but exacerbated those inequities which I briefly address below, although the full impacts are not yet known. One of the most immediate concerns has been the accessibility of emergency updates to people with various types of disabilities (Hanifie, 2020). Equally concerning is that people with disabilities face a greater risk of being denied access to treatment: there are reports of people with disabilities dying after being denied medical treatment (Flanders, 2020). Access to support services because of restricted travel and social distancing measures means that many people with disabilities are denied basic care at home (CBC, 2020).

The Global Action on Disability Network (2020) has expressed concerns about the growing inequities in education due to limited accessibility and access to resources during the COVID-19 pandemic. Girls with disabilities are particularly vulnerable to being cut out of education. Amidst growing concerns, Women Enabled International (2020) conducted a survey into the gaps in addressing the needs of women with disabilities during the pandemic. Increased risk of violence, barriers to accessing health and reproductive health services, loss of income and supports, and meeting basic needs were all urgent issues among the women with disabilities who responded to the survey.

As part of my research, I endeavoured to reach participants in various countries to understand more about these efforts and what keeps them going. I ask: 'What is it about this work that keeps people motivated and hopeful?', 'What challenges do they face?', and 'Why do they push past those challenges?' There are several factors to consider in this analysis; family life, political context, cultural context, resources, safety, individual circumstances to name but a few. What are the commonalities and differences among community organizers? What role does perception of self and others play? I followed each of these questions through my research in order to understand the effects of oppression and the challenges it poses. My project asks, 'Under what conditions do movements for women and trans people with disabilities emerge?' I propose that movements to end violence can transform individual and collective consciousness about disability and gender oppression. I investigate what this transformative process looks like.

In this chapter, I work through concepts of intersectionality, oppression, and consciousness as being critical to understanding elements of transformation. In *Pedagogy of the Oppressed* (1970), Brazilian educator Paolo Freire contributed a great deal to our understanding of oppression, particularly the dynamics between the oppressed and the oppressor in moving towards liberation and freedom through solidarity building.

James Charlton wrote *Nothing About Us Without Us* in 1998. His research involved interviewing more than 50 disability rights activists in 13 countries over 10 years. His work explores in great detail disability oppression, resistance to it, and empowerment. While his work does address violence against people with disabilities, it does not address gender-based violence. I, therefore, draw connections to other scholars as needed.

In 1963, social psychologist Erving Goffman wrote *Stigma* in which he defined stigma as an attribute that discredits a person and defines them as unusual. He makes the distinction that only those undesirable traits which do not fit our stereotype of what a person should be are stigmatized. His work offered insight into interactions between stigmatized and non-stigmatized individuals as well as into the psyche of the stigmatized person. This is important to my theoretical framework because my starting point for looking at false consciousness and the conditions leading to it is the influence of negative perceptions of disability.

The contributions of these scholars are not complete as they do not fully account for the experiences of diverse groups of people. While critical to our understanding of oppression, their theories do not account for intersecting identities and forms of oppression. To address this gap, I incorporate contributions from critical race studies, critical legal studies, women and gender studies, and disability studies into my theoretical framework. First though, I want to address intersectionality as a thread that will run throughout this book.

## Intersectionality

Angela Davis (1983), in exploring tensions between abolition and suffrage movements, explained that Black women who lived at a time when abolition and women's suffrage were being fought for found themselves unable to separate parts of their identity in order to fit into one movement or the other. People in each of these movements had difficulty understanding that the issues were connected. As Audre Lorde says, 'There is no such thing as a single-issue struggle because we do not live single-issue lives' (1983: 138).

As noted in the introduction, the term 'intersectionality' was coined by Kimberlé Crenshaw in her 1989 work examining antidiscrimination law and the ways in which the court system failed to recognize how the intersectional identities of Black women in the United States contributed to their discrimination. She used the analogy of discrimination being like traffic at an intersection; it may flow from many directions, increasing the risk of injury or harm, and it is at the intersection of this traffic where discrimination takes place.

Intersectionality is important for understanding oppression. Privilege and oppression are complex. We may experience privilege based on systems that support one aspect of our identity while also experiencing oppression within systems that disadvantage us based on another aspect of our identity. We may uphold systems that create someone else's oppression while at the same time identifying oppressive systems to challenge in our own lives. A good example of this is the way in which white feminists have historically failed to understand the privilege of being white because of a focus on oppression as women. Patricia Collins has argued that,

> Although most individuals have little difficulty identifying their own victimization within some major system of oppression – whether it be by race, social class, religion, physical ability, sexual orientation, ethnicity, age or gender – they typically fail to see how their thoughts and actions uphold someone else's subordination. Thus white feminists routinely point with confidence to their oppression as women but resist seeing how much their white skin privileges them. (2000: 287)

In discussing intersectionality, my focus is not on identity markers, rather it is on the structures that rely on those identity markers to privilege or disadvantage groups of people. Instead of naming the various aspects or characteristics that comprise our identities, intersectionality recognizes the systems, structures, and norms that create multiple disadvantage and discrimination, sometimes offering up one issue at the expense of others.

We talk about intersectionality, then, to get at issues of oppression. Our experiences are shaped and informed by our identity. When those experiences are negative or harmful, solutions come from our understanding of the root causes, whether these are structural, societal, or cultural. Intersectionality further plays a diagnostic role in identifying those structures that produce marginalization by treating experiences of marginalized people as valid and as a source of knowledge production (Falcón and Nash, 2015).

Intersectionality, as a theory, is never done and has the potential to address new issues or power structures as they emerge (Carbado et al., 2013). Enter disability as part of identity. Critical disability studies emerged in the 1970s (Meekosha and Shuttleworth, 2009) but its intersection with other aspects of identity still requires further analysis. Barnes and Mercer (2010) compare groups of oppressed people when, in fact, these groups are not mutually exclusive sets of people who always experience oppression based on a single trait such as gender or disability. Instead, individuals simultaneously comprise various traits which makes comparing groups insufficient. Instead, oppression must be understood as affecting different people in different ways depending on their social, economic, cultural, racial, gender, and ability locations.

A growing number of researchers have begun to advocate for intersectional approaches within critical disability studies (Goethals et al., 2015) and the disability movement (Bê, 2012; de Silva de Alwis, 2009). Some argue that the growing focus on intersectionality has created potential for political alliances between critical disability studies and critical race or feminist discourses (Meekosha and Shuttleworth, 2009).

It is just as important for trans studies, disability studies, and feminism to align in their commitment to a truly intersectional approach. Slater and Liddiard have argued that,

> Just as Disability Studies has been accused of being male-centric, feminism has often excluded disabled women's experiences (Garland-Thomson, 2011). Similar criticisms have been levelled at Trans Studies. Krell (2017) critiques Serano's (2007, 2013) work for silently centering white, middle-class trans women. Trans Studies has also omitted to include experiences of disablism and ableism – and often Disability Studies has been cisnormative (Baril, 2015; Withers, 2013). The role of Feminist Disability Studies, therefore, is not just to add disabled women's experiences to those of non-disabled women; nor to create another discrete form of feminism (2018: 87).

Social policies are an important consideration, given that much of our daily lives is governed by them, whether they be health care, violence prevention initiatives, poverty reduction, or income support. Understanding and prioritizing intersectional frameworks is critical to providing relevant and responsive services for women and trans people with disabilities and those experiencing gender-based violence. Citing the work of Ferree, Hankivsky (2012) cautions that by addressing inequities for some groups other groups may be disadvantaged because inequalities are often mutually constitutive. Intersectional analysis, then, can mitigate the risks by addressing power relations which maintain inequities.

In terms of intersectionality as a process, I suggest here that there are core elements of an intersectional approach which are central to and inform how I approach this research and interpret my findings. Hankivsky identifies eight central tenets in a collection she terms an *Intersectionality Based Policy Analysis Framework* (2012). Though the principles are designed for a policy analysis they are a useful guide for work that addresses multiple markers of identity and oppression. These principles are: A) recognizing intersecting categories; B) multi-level analysis; C) power; D) reflexivity; E) understanding time and space; F) valuing diverse knowledges; G) social justice; and H) equity.

Experiences of gender-based violence in the disability community are shaped by intersecting social relations of power based on various identity characteristics. Intersectional analysis recognizes **intersecting categories** of identity because identity is more complex than a sum of individual effects. 'Intersectionality conceptualizes social categories as interacting with and co-constituting one another to create unique social locations that vary according to time and place' (Hankivsky, 2012: 35). In examining the experiences of women of colour with disabilities, Erevelles and Minear refer to McCall's inter-categorical framework of intersectionality because, in addition to situating the experiences of women of colour at the intersection of multiple categories, it 'describes the structural conditions within which these social categories are constructed by, and intermeshed with each other in specific historical contexts' (Erevelles and Minear, 2013: 357). It is these intersections and their effects that are important to intersectional analysis.

**Multi-level** analysis is the second principle of an intersectional analysis which seeks to understand experiences 'between and across various levels of society' (Hankivsky, 2012: 35), including the global, national, provincial, regional, community, grassroots, and individual levels. The relationships between structures and social locations are revealed through intersectional analysis.

The exploration of **power** dynamics is critical to understanding oppression and gender-based violence in the disability community. There are three particular considerations here that leave us with a lot to unpack:

> i) power operates at discursive and structural levels to exclude particular knowledges and experiences (Foucault, 1977); ii) subject positions and categories (e.g., 'race') are constructed and shaped by processes and systems of power (e.g. racialization and racism); and iii) these processes operate together to shape experiences of privilege and penalty between and among groups (Collins, 2000) (Hankivsky, 2012: 35).

**Reflexivity** is a fourth principle that helps an intersectional analysis to address power dynamics by acknowledging its importance in all areas of life.

Reflexivity recognizes power within oneself and also in relationship to others. 'The transformative potential of reflexivity is found within practices that bring critical self-awareness, role-awareness, interrogation of power and privilege, and the questioning of assumptions and "truths" in policy processes (Clark, 2012)' (Hankivsky, 2012: 36).

Intersectional analysis acknowledges that our experiences are not rigid; instead, when and where we live interacts with what we know about the world. **Time and space**, the fifth principle of intersectional analysis, recognizes the ways in which our lived experiences are heavily influenced by our social position and location. This means that the way we understand the world, and even our experiences, are subject to change, 'Thus, time and space are not static, fixed or objective dimensions and/or processes, but are fluid, changeable and experienced through our interpretations, senses and feelings, which are, in turn, heavily conditioned by our social positioning/location, among other factors (Tuan, 1977)' (Hankivsky, 2012: 37).

Similarly, the sixth principle of **diverse knowledge**, particularly from those who are marginalized or excluded, is central to an intersectional analysis which is concerned with addressing the relationship between power and knowledge production. Hankivsky says that this type of analysis 'expands understandings of what is typically constituted as "evidence" by recognizing a diversity of knowledges, paradigms and theoretical perspectives that can be included in policy analysis, such as knowledge generated from qualitative or quantitative research; empirical or interpretive data; and Indigenous knowledges' (2012: 37).

The seventh principle is **social justice** and it is emphasized within inter-sectional analysis for its focus on equity. Hankivsky argues that 'Theories of social justice frequently challenge inequities at their source and require the interrogation of complex social and power relations' (2012: 38).

Closely related to social justice is the final principle of **equity**, which is concerned with fairness. Equity is not to be confused with equality. Equality is about treating everyone the same, whereas equity means giving everyone what they need to succeed. Buettgen notes that 'Equality also aims to promote fairness, but it can only work if everyone starts from the same place and needs the same help' (2018: 31). Hankivsky, though, reminds us of the distinction between equity and equality in terms of outcomes which are also important: 'Where inequality may refer to any measurable difference in outcomes of interest, inequities exist where those differences are unfair or unjust' (2012: 38). Working through this research project, I have kept these principles in mind, and they are referred to throughout this book.

In part, this book is concerned with how disability, gender, and other aspects of identity shape experiences of oppression. The next sections examine oppression theory, exploring the material conditions of oppression, and what we mean when we talk about false consciousness, raised consciousness, and, finally, empowered consciousness. These are core elements of resistance to oppression and provide the theoretical foundation of this work.

## Material conditions of oppression

### *What is oppression?*

As noted in the introduction, Iris Marion Young (1990) identifies five manifes-tations of oppression: exploitation, marginalization, powerlessness, cultural imperialism, and violence. I want to take some time now to explore these concepts because they offer an insightful way to think about oppression–which is often an abstract concept – through considering the lived experiences that result from oppression. Young discussed these terms in relation to labour which is a useful approach because, as will become clear, there is an economic component to oppression that helps to sustain it.

Young defines **exploitation** as the use of people's labour for profit without fair compensation. In a capitalist system, the haves exploit the have-nots. The transfer of energy from one group to another such that one group benefits at the expense of another is a manifestation of oppression. Women, for example, have traditionally done domestic forms of labour for the benefit of men without much benefit in return. Exploitation can take other forms not addressed by Young. Women with disabilities, for example, may be sexually exploited by their partners or caregivers. They experience physical, sexual, and emotional abuse, and are at risk of having resources taken or withheld from them by family members or caregivers.

**Marginalization** is the process of pushing a group of people to a lower social status or to the margins of society. The marginalized group becomes excluded so that not even their labour is wanted. Their marginalization and resulting social exclusion, Young argues, is dangerous because it can lead to 'severe material deprivation and even extermination' (1990: 50). Women with disabilities experience marginalization when they are denied access to services or jobs, or when they are hidden from their communities by family members because of their disability. They are often viewed as asexual or incapable of close or romantic relationships, which also leads to denial of motherhood. There has been an erasure of trans people with disabilities as is evident from the absence of their experiences in much of the work done to address gender-based violence and disability. This is due, in part, to the fact that people with disabilities are desexualized, hypersexualized, or treated as heterosexual (Slater and Liddiard, 2018).

**Powerlessness** is the domination of one group who give orders to others who have no decision-making powers. People who experience powerlessness may think so little of themselves that they do not even realise they are oppressed (Freire, 1970). Three features of powerlessness, according to Young (1990), are the inability to develop one's capacity, a lack of decision-making power (Young was referring to decision-making in the workplace, but power-lessness extends to decisions around personal care, interacting with others, family life, and relationships), and being treated disrespectfully because of one's social status. Young points out that these first three forms of oppression are concerned with structures, institutions, and relations of power related to the division of labour. Being denied the opportunity to be in relationships or to have children is one form of powerlessness. Forced institutionalization and forced sterilization are clear systemic manifestations of powerlessness. These practices affect material conditions in such a way that some benefit while others are expendable.

**Cultural imperialism** refers to the process whereby the culture of the ruling class dominates as the norm, resulting in a process of Othering. The dominant group's perspective is then used to interpret their experiences and those of other groups. In this case, differences become viewed as deviance or inferiority. Young says, 'The culturally dominated undergo a paradoxical oppression, in that they are both marked out by stereotypes and at the same time rendered invisible' (1990: 59). People with disabilities are dominated by norms related to the most intimate aspects of our lives, bodies, and minds. We are marked by stereotypes of normalcy in a society that still prefers not to see us. The focus here is on systemic causes of oppression: the stereotypes and prejudices embedded in our societal, institutional, and political practices.

**Violence** takes the form of humiliation and harm which is unpredictable causing the oppressed group to become fearful of random attacks. It is more than experiencing actual acts of violence, but the knowledge that one is always at risk of violence without provocation. Young (1990) believes the troubling part is that it is the social context surrounding violence that makes it possible and, in some cases, acceptable. Systems of injustice that do little to prevent or punish violence are cause for concern. Women and trans people with disabilities are at constant risk of violence whether it is interpersonal, structural, or pertaining to socio-economic location. I say socio-economic location because women and trans people with disabilities who are unable to perform in standard ways may be prone to income instability in often convoluted policy landscapes that do very little to support them in a meaningful and consistent way. If they rely upon a partner for economic support, leaving in the face of violence may be even more challenging.

## What contributes to disability oppression?

Disability oppression is complex. It is a foundational component of my work and research and has been my entry point into exploring gender and disability consciousness. Charlton (1998) identifies the political economy, negative attitudes about disability, and psychological internalization or false consciousness about disability as contributing to disability oppression. I will address each of these separately.

### Political economy

The bi-directional link between poverty and disability is well established (ADD International, 2017; ILO, 2015; Beisland and Mersland, 2014; WHO and

World Bank, 2011). Participation in economic activities is lower for people with disabilities. Accessibility to the labour market, financial services, capital, microfinance institutions, and groups for people with disabilities is hindered by the lack of physically accessible spaces, insufficient communication accommodations such as sign language interpreters, and attitudinal barriers due to misconceptions that people with disabilities are a burden and incapable of contributing to the labour market (Seifert and Goldstein, 2016; ILO, 2015; Beisland and Mersland, 2014). These realities extend to other areas of life – school, home, or social settings – and contribute to disability oppression.

Critical legal theory offers an important element to understanding oppression. Access to legal recourse and realizing our rights is important to achieving equality and equity. In terms of how our societies are organized, we are governed by states which are politically organized. The material conditions of our lives are reflected in the political economy. The law governs relationships between civil society and the state. The law, then, through its influencing of the state and the political economy, has the power to emancipate and the power to place barriers to that emancipation (Christodoulidis, 2019). Additionally, the law itself is not applied in a vacuum: legal outcomes are determined by political and social contexts and, frankly, the people operating within these systems. This framing is important because it takes power dynamics into account, understanding that the law reflects class interests and relations of power (Hosking, 2008).

The impact of the political economy is also gendered. Economic oppression is included within my work on violence as a long-recognized issue taken up by feminist and critical race studies for its part in upholding a capitalist system (Kennedy, 2008; Arat-Koc, 2006; de Beauvoir, 1949:2011; Eisenstein, 1999; Bannerji, 1995). Marx (1867) observed that the nature of the capitalist system requires a reserve army of labour on hand to accommodate the inevitable rapid expansion in production. In *Sister Outsider* (1984), antiracist feminist theorist Audre Lorde expands on Marx's ideas. She identifies exploitation of difference as necessary to uphold capitalism. In a capitalist system, the profit economy relies on surplus outsiders in times of overproduction. Lorde argues that the rejection of difference is therefore necessary. She also says that, when responding to difference, people can choose to: 1) ignore it, if it is not a perceived threat; 2) copy it, if it appears to dominate; or 3) destroy it, if it is perceived as subordinate. So, by its very nature capitalism exploits and oppresses difference.

Similarly, colonialism relies on difference. If the colonized are too unlike the colonizer, they must be dominated; and yet the colonized will never be fully integrated because then they would be equal and no longer in need of colonizing (Smith, 2005). Difference becomes a threat to the dominant group because it is difference that has shaped power relations in favour of colonial, patriarchal, capitalist domination. For example, I think it is important to acknowledge that colonialism effectively established a patriarchy among Canadian Indigenous people by reorganizing their social relations so that women became dominated by male agreements with the colonizer (Million, 2013).

These issues are part of an important history that still impacts the political economy today. It also provides the context for the systems within which people work to end oppression. These oppressive systems have negative outcomes. Indigenous people with disabilities, for example, face unique rights violations, particularly related to access to services and the right to independent living. The Permanent Forum on Indigenous Issues identifies a major form of discrimination for Indigenous people with disabilities as the lack of available quality services compared to other people with disabilities (United Nations, 2013). Indigenous people seeking disability supports in Canada are often shuffled between various levels of government due to jurisdictional funding issues. These funding issues are exacerbated when a person leaves a reserve (Durst et al., 2006).

If you are an Indigenous woman with a disability in Canada, you face a complex policy landscape when accessing disability supports, health care, childcare, income support, employment, or other services that are provincially supplied for non-Indigenous people but fall under federal jurisdiction for Indigenous people. Another concern is that when Indigenous women use litigation and the court system to address the injustices against them and seek equality, they are often pitted against not only the Canadian government but also their communities and other Indigenous women. Some in their communities may view them as acting against self-government. The division so created supports the manifestation of the colonial, patriarchal influence that further oppresses Indigenous women (McIvor, 2004).

Disability scholars have also pointed to the marginalization of women with disabilities as a consequence of socio-historic and material conditions of capitalist, patriarchal states and broader structural oppression as evidenced by an inadequate state response pertaining to programmes and services for women with disabilities (Erevelles, 2011; Malacrida, 2010; Muthukrishna et al., 2009; Mays, 2006). Cultural imperialism, as a form of oppression, is always at play.

### Negative attitudes

The second contribution to oppression that Charlton identifies is negative attitudes about disability. Before industrialization and globalization, societies were organized to be self-sufficient and family members were assigned tasks according to their capabilities. The advancement of technology and industry has meant less self-sufficiency, leaving people with disabilities to be viewed as a burden to their communities. The charity model of the early twentieth century served to perpetuate views that people with disabilities are in need of help (Price, 2011). The medical model of disability, which treated disability as an individual medical issue in need of fixing, followed (Oliver, 1990). Though the 1980s saw a paradigm shift in thinking about disability as socially constructed (Finkelstein, 2001; Oliver, 1997), there is still a perceived biological inferiority assigned to people with disabilities (Loja et. al. 2013; Abberley, 1987).

Negative perceptions of disability can also be seen in the way the law has historically treated, or not, people with disabilities (Roeher Institute, 1995). Take, for example, women who were declared 'criminally insane' in Canada. In the early nineteenth century, it was not uncommon for penitentiaries and asylums to shuffle patients back and forth because they were seen as burdens (Roman et al., 2009; Kendall, 1999; Kelm, 1992; Mitchinson, 1987). The harsh, inhumane, and unjustifiable conditions under which women were histori-cally declared criminally insane is beyond the scope of this book except to say that forcible confinement in prisons or institutions was also used as a way to control Indigenous populations during colonization (Menzies and Palys, 2006). Eugenics policies and sterilization laws further reflect the negative perceptions of disability.

Alison Kafer (2013) explores the case of Ashley X, a young girl with disabil-ities, whose parents sought growth attenuation and sterilization procedures for their daughter, arguing that changing her body in this way would allow them to care for her at home more easily and for a longer period of time. There are assumptions about quality of life that are held in making decisions like this. Kafer explains that doctors justified their decision to carry out the procedures, despite the absence of a court order, as a means of avoiding eventual institutionalization. The treatment, though, does not guarantee that Ashley will never be institutionalized. It has been argued that these treatments happen because there are no social supports available for parents of children with disabilities. Quality of life is usually described as though it is evident in the appearance or diagnosis, and always includes level of functioning and pain. But level of functioning might be lower than one's ability if one does not have access to the resources needed to improve function. Quality of life is then a function of access to resources, and measuring that access is ambiguous and contradictory. Drawing lines between levels of impairment for the purpose of making treatment decisions "suggests that some people are more deserving of ethical concern and consideration than others" (Kafer, 2013: 64). Ashley X was considered too severely disabled to be considered a disabled person; her parents referred to her as 'permanently unabled' in order to distinguish her from other disabled people. The consequences of this are that her experience becomes invisible. Kafer further argues:

> If crip theory and critical disability studies remind us to attend not only to the experiences of disabled people but also, and especially, to the ways in which disability and ability work in the world, then we need to contest this representation of some minds and bodies as beyond the reach of disability analysis and activism (2013: 67).

If functioning becomes a measure of effectiveness, lower functioning equates to defectiveness which is then in need of cure. Eli Clare tells us that

"Defectiveness wields incredible power because ableism builds and maintains the notion that defective body-minds are undesirable, worthless, disposable, or in need of cure" (2017: 23). And therefore defectiveness holds value in an ableist world. Clare (2017) adds, 'The ableist invention of defectiveness functions as an indisputable justification not only for cure but also for many systems of oppression' (2017: 23).

Negative perceptions of disability can impact the way the law is applied, and this does little to help address oppression. Even when there are laws to protect people from mistreatment, they are not evenly applied. In the case of Ashley X, the hospital performed sterilization without a court order; they later agreed to not carry out this procedure on other children with disabilities without first having a court order (Kafer, 2013). Societal perceptions of disability cannot be legislated. For instance, in thinking about the Convention on the Rights of Persons with Disabilities, Hoefmans and de Beco say that 'overcoming cultural and attitudinal barriers may remain to be one of the major challenges in ensuring the concrete implementation of the CRPD [Convention on the Rights of Persons with Disabilities]' (2010: 13).

The media also plays a distinct role in reflecting and perpetuating perceptions of disability (Schwartz et al., 2010; Titchkosky, 2005; Haller and Ralph, 2002). The importance of this should not be underestimated. With frequent exposure to media messages related to self-identity, individuals may internalize what they observe from mass media and project that information to their own values (Zhang and Haller, 2013). Disability has been historically portrayed in media as monstrous and threatening, heroic, inspirational, or pitiful (Nelson, 2011; Barnes, 1992).

Difference based on disability is viewed so negatively that denying a person's disability or acting as though one does not see a disability can be construed as a compliment. At the other end of the perception spectrum is the gaze that is often directed toward people with disabilities. The gaze is different to simply looking: the gaze assigns meaning to what is being seen. Hughes (1999) tells us that impairment is constructed by the non-disabled gaze, rendering people with disabilities as strangers and Othered. What is considered normative goes unquestioned while those who do not fit become strangers or outsiders.

Garland-Thomson (2006) offers a different approach and frames these interactions in terms of staring. She separates staring from the gaze, choosing to focus not on power but on the visual social relationship. She tells us that staring in its basic form is looking at something or someone for the time it takes to understand what we are seeing, particularly when it is unexpected. She argues that the staring interaction is always fraught with meaning. Garland-Thomson identifies three types of stares: *arrested* – usually derived from surprised and confused responses or gawking; *separated* – whereas the arrested stare may cause a person to stop, the separated stare is one that does not halt the starer but rather causes them to look over their shoulder and perhaps experience revulsion; and the *engaged stare* – this is laden with the intention to know, making it perhaps the most intrusive.

The second way staring is fraught with meaning is that the onus for managing the staring relationship primarily falls on the person being stared at (Garland-Thomson, 2006). Why is this important? Hughes (1999) highlights Sartre's argument that there is a loss of power for the person subjected to the gaze. The male gaze, medical gaze, and colonial gaze create interactions that come with the possibility to resist them.

I want to now discuss the rhetoric that informs our perceptions. As already noted, women with disabilities experience additional negative attitudes about their sexuality and their reproductive lives; they are often infantilized and treated as though they are incapable of being sexual beings or effective mothers. Sometimes women will have their children taken away or experience sexual abuse because of their perceived vulnerability (Muthukrishna et. al, 2009).

Women with disabilities have been described as at a 'double disadvantage,' and this framing has been critiqued for ignoring the role of non-disabled people and oppressive structures in contributing to their oppression. Employing a double disadvantage analysis turns women with disabilities into passive victims. Jenny Morris explains: 'I don't think that I, or many other disabled women, want to read of non-disabled researchers analysing how awful our lives are because we "suffer from" two modes of oppression' (1993: 163). This analysis is interesting because it raises questions about empowerment and the importance of non-disabled feminists questioning their assumptions of disability. The feminist movement took issue with framing women as passive victims and were instead outraged about the powerlessness women experienced in relation to men. The feminist and disability movements did not show much overlap at that time. Disability was commonly an add-on in the early feminist movement (Morris, 1991, 1993). In fact, historically, feminists were reluctant to include women with disabilities because they did not want to risk tarnishing the image of women as strong and independent (Price, 2011). The experiences of trans women have been historically excluded from feminist and disability studies. There have been recent calls to create stronger alliances between these disciplines (Slater and Liddiard, 2018).

Goffman (1963) argued that the stigmatized person is often perceived as not quite human, and Freire (1970) argued that this dehumanization is a necessary process for oppression to occur. He said that when people are alienated from their own decision-making, they move from subjects to objects. Freire considers the impact of this dehumanization on the oppressed and argues that they internalize their own understanding of themselves based on what they are told by those who hold power over them. Andre Lorde reminds us of the relentlessness of dehumanization:

> it is easier once again for white women to believe the dangerous fantasy that if you are good enough, pretty enough, sweet enough, quiet enough, teach the children to behave, hate the right people, and marry the right

men, then you will be allowed to co-exist with patriarchy in relative peace, at least until a man needs your job or the neighbourhood rapist happens along. And true, unless one lives and loves in the trenches it is difficult to remember that the war against dehumanization is ceaseless (1984: 119).

This will be important later when we talk about resisting oppression.

The third component of oppression, for Charlton, is false consciousness and the internalized oppression linked to that. I turn to these aspects now.

## False consciousness and internalized oppression

In terms of power, the self-regulation that ensues from an awareness of the gaze has been taken up by disability scholars (Dawn, 2014) and this will surely affect perception. In fact, Goffman offers insightful analysis of how these processes, along with the weight of managing these interactions, influence the stigmatized person's self-perception: 'Given that the stigmatized individual in our society acquires identity standards which he applies to himself in spite of failing to conform to them, it is inevitable that he will feel some ambivalence about his own self' (1963: 106). He goes on to say that when people see someone like themselves acting in a stereotypical way, this can create negative feelings. At the same time, they identify with what disturbs them, so they feel ashamed. Then they feel ashamed about feeling ashamed. What he says happens is that a person will then not embrace their group, but nor do they let it go.

As Loja et. al posit:

> The non-disabled gaze or ableist point of view is also driven by curiosity, perceived as a 'right' to intrude, inquire, appropriate impairment as a public spectacle ... The gaze is the medium through which ableism invalidates the impaired body and at the same time sustains its own authenticity (2013: 194).

That repeated staring can lead to negative self-perceptions was also found in a Renwick et. al. (2018) study with men with acquired spinal cord injury. They found that the men in the study often felt discouraged from participating in society as a result of staring. The findings were not straightforward, however, because some reported that over time they felt more dehumanized while others, if they were able to perceive the staring as coming from a place of interest or curiosity, were more comfortable with their social interactions and even engaged in opportunities to reframe their disability. Furthermore, when people with disabilities experience the gaze in public it can create a distancing between disabled people just as it can create distance between people with disabilities and those without (Loja et at. 2013).

*Internalized oppression* First and foremost, Marks (1999) tells us that internalized oppression is most effective when we do not realize it is there. Experiences might be so painful that we cannot consciously experience them and yet they affect our self-esteem as well as our thoughts and behaviour.

Williams, who could find no existing framework for internalized oppression, frames oppression in terms of dominant, subordinate, and border groups. Further, and relevant to my current project, Williams says:

> Belonging to multiple social groups means that every human has the potential to belong to dominant and subordinate groups simultaneously, thereby experiencing both privilege based on some identities and disadvantage based on other identities ... oppression is not experienced based solely on membership in one social group; rather, it is mediated by the combination of all of one's identities (2012: 20).

Goffman (1963) offers the possibility that stigmatized people may feel uncertain about how others will react to them and will concern themselves with the impressions they make, in a similar way to the self-regulation discussed above. These worries are reasonable given that strangers will often feel justified or entitled to engage in conversations about the perceived stigma; conversations that would not be had with what Goffman calls 'normal' individuals. Being subjected to unwanted conversations about one's body, movement, and behaviour, I would argue, creates a sense in the person that their presence is disrupting the norm. How one internalizes this, whether it is to resist the power dynamics imposed upon one, or to navigate them without protest, is important because this will impact experiences of oppression.

Charlton (1998) says that psychological internalization creates a false consciousness through various means. First, it causes people with disabilities to believe the lies they are told about themselves. Stereotypes of disability in mass media have also been shown to affect self-perceptions. Being exposed to negative portrayals of disability has been associated with corresponding negative self-perceptions within the disability community (Zhang and Haller, 2013). Negative stereotypes lead to feelings of self-pity, self-hate, shame, and negative self-worth (Galvin, 2005; Marks, 1999).

Second, these feelings obscure what is really possible for the person and also what the source of their oppression really is. Charlton says, 'They cannot recognize that their self-perceived pitiful lives are simply a perverse mirroring of a pitiful world order. In this regard people with disabilities have much in common with others who also have internalized their own oppression' (1998: 27). This is important because false consciousness is simultaneously a fundamental source of oppression and a barrier to advancing the disability rights movement. Identifying how internalization occurs for an individual may help us understand who will resist oppression (Charlton, 1998).

Critical race scholars have been central to developing a complex understanding of internalized oppression. They have attributed internalized oppression to stereotypical representations of race and gender that serve white patriarchal systems, particularly through film which reflects culture, reimagines it, and also creates it. This, in turn, according to hooks (1996), has led to an internalized way of Black people seeing themselves and the world. Other scholars have added that internalized oppression is seen through efforts of the oppressed to be more like the oppressor for fear of being lower on the hierarchy (see Lorde, 1984; Davis, 1983). Lorde says that this fear plays out in the minds of the oppressed in the following way: 'I must attack you first before our enemies confuse us with each other but they will anyway.' (1984: 169). This articulation insightfully delves into the psyche of the oppressed woman.

Let us talk about freedom. Freedom is important for empowerment, but it also poses challenges in the psyche of the oppressed. Specifically, I want to talk about freedom and its importance to social movements. Here I draw specifically on the work of Black feminists because they brought to the fore much of what we now understand about the complexities of oppression and social movements.

Freedom is not just the absence of coercion. Of course, this is a necessary condition for freedom, but it is not sufficient. In order to be free, one must have the resources available to make decisions that affect one's life. Anything less than this is violent. Freedom has been taken up in critical race scholarship through a thorough examination of Black women's liberation movements. There has been a fear of turning silence into language because, as an act of self-revelation, this can be dangerous for Black women; but to remain silent is also dangerous (Lorde, 1984). Freedom is understood, not as something that must be divided among oppressed people, but rather it is something that must be collectively pursued so that everyone attains it. This has been a challenge to social movement organizing. We know that the women's liberation movement has been racist (hooks, 1996; Davis, 1983) and ableist (Morris, 1993). In this sense, it is important that oppression research encompasses all people in pursuit of the struggle for such freedoms (Lorde, 1984).

Additionally, it has been argued that powerlessness is the strongest form of oppression (Young, 1990; Freire, 1970). If one feels powerless, then this may lead one to passively accept one's circumstances. Goffman (1962) argued that oppression is more easily enacted when denial of its occurrence is fed through conformity, thereby removing autonomy.

Consider the ways in which people with disabilities have been discriminated against through the various systems that should ensure autonomy and self-determination. Legal systems are not value free, nor are they neutral. Legal definitions of disability possibly serve to protect, but they also regulate and exclude (Kanter, 2011). People with disabilities have long had their rights to autonomy violated through sexual sterilization laws. Even after such laws have been repealed, case law permitting sterilization continues (Rioux and Patton, 2011). Case law around things like consent and capacity, genetic testing, and institutionalization only serves to further the powerlessness and negative perceptions people with disabilities experience. Freire (1970) argues that, when oppressed, the powerless can fear freedom; this is problematic because liberation must be pursued constantly and consistently.

Turning back to internalized oppression, Barnes and Mercer (2010) draw on Abberley's 1987 work that distinguishes the biological experience of people with disabilities from women or racialized people. Unlike sex or skin colour, impairment encompasses functional limitation which is itself a part of the social oppression. Functional limitations are framed as defects and, as Clare points out,

> Entire body-minds, communities, cultures are squeezed into defective. And then that single blunt concept turns, becoming defect. Bullies hurl it as an insult. Strangers ask it out of curiosity. Doctors note it in medical files. Judges and juries hear it in testimony. Scientists study it as truth. Politicians write it into policy. Defect and defective explode with hate, power, and control (2017: 26).

Barnes and Mercer (2010) argue that, like women and people of colour, people with disabilities have historically experienced oppression based on biological arguments. The interesting thing about disability is that, unlike other aspects of identity, disability is the only category for which the negative effects are not necessarily socially constructed. If the physical environment were accessible, and social structures did not present barriers to people with disabilities, some uncomfortable or painful aspects of disability would still exist. The disability movement has long resisted acknowledging these aspects for fear of contributing to negative perceptions of disability and this impacts forms of oppression:

> Women and men may be physiologically and psychologically different, but it is no longer possible to argue that women are made less capable by their biology ... Similarly, only racists would see the biological differences between ethnic communities as the explanation for their social differences. Nor is it clear why being lesbian or gay would put any individual at a disadvantage, in the absence of prejudice and discrimination. But even in the absence of social barriers or oppression, it would still be problematic to have an impairment, because many impairments are limiting or difficult, not neutral (Shakespeare, 2006: 41).

The truth is that sometimes disability is painful, uncomfortable, or confusing but this should not be equated to a lower quality of life or lesser value. Morris (1991) says that we need the courage to say when there are awful things or when there are things in which to have pride about having a disability. Non-disabled people make judgements about our lives as people with disabilities and so there is a reluctance to talk about all of the realities of disability. The consequences then become that we do not feel entitled to talk about how we really feel when our experiences with disability are not positive. This silence tells both disabled and non-disabled people that disability is undesirable. These negative stereotypes and attitudes about disability become internalized and create various impacts on the self-esteem of people with disabilities (Putnam, 2005). Taking up the disability identity, then, for many has meant adopting a negatively constructed characteristic. Scholars writing about oppression have said that internalized patterns of oppression are something that must be exposed in order to move towards social change (Charlton, 1998; Lorde, 1984).

## Raised consciousness

Self-identifying as part of a disability community is not easy when, for a long time, there has been no history to which to refer (Charlton, 1998). If it has not been written about or acknowledged, how can one even imagine what a disability community looks like? There are a few factors that have contributed to this historical lack of community: isolation, diversity, and the domination of the medical model of disability have made it difficult to move toward community formation.

First, people with disabilities have historically been scattered or isolated at home and away from their communities. If we do not grow up with people like us then, it stands to reason, our locations are varied and unpredictable. True, some people with disabilities grow up in a natural community of others with similar characteristics related to disability, but the vast array of experiences for people with disabilities makes it difficult to point to a cohesive group identity based on disability (Asch, 2001).

This leads me to the second point: people with disabilities comprise diverse and sometimes overlapping or semi-contradictory identities (Charlton, 1998). And, while disability is socially constructed (Finkelstein, 2001; Oliver, 1990), the characteristics of disability have describable effects (Vehmas and Watson, 2014; Shakespeare, 2006; Asch, 2001) which vary from person to person. These variations depend not only on impairment, but also on how impairment interacts with the physical environment (if at all), and on how the impairment is perceived.

Third, the disability community has been historically dominated by the medical profession making it hard to develop a strong sense of community among people with disabilities (Asch, 2001).

There is not a long-existing disability culture passed down through stories or customs. This means that, historically, people with disabilities have obtained knowledge from non-disabled culture (Morris, 1999; Barnartt, 1996; Charlton, 1998). Sometimes people with disabilities will go through much of their life not seeing anyone else that looks like them. Goffman (1963) says, though, that even when contact with other similar individuals is limited, it is often sufficient to simply show someone that other similar people exist. Perhaps it is in those fleeting moments to which Goffman referred that the foundations for consciousness-raising begin. Charlton argued that individual consciousness is not fixed; it 'is contingent on factors such as intelligence, curiosity, character, personality, experience, and chance; political-economic and cultural structures (class, race, gender, disability, age, sexual preference); and social institutions' (1998: 28–29). It is always evolving (Collins, 2000).

### Disability consciousness among women and trans people with disabilities

The empowering effects of a changed consciousness have been surfaced by critical race theorists (Collins, 2000) and, without calling it so, Morris (1991) drew her attention to individual consciousness of women with disabilities as the starting place for liberation from prejudices. Meekosha (2002) argues that there is a complex relationship between identity formation and collective action which is important to understanding the movement and the political activism of women with disabilities. She further emphasizes the importance of narrative in advancing the contributions of women with disabilities to a wider social movement. These narratives must be honest about personal growth, struggles, pain, and affirmation as distinct contributions of women with disabilities.

> Identity formation for individual women emerges through action in the world and responses from the world. Thus women with impairments, whose life experiences have often been traumatic, and who see only negative reflections of themselves in their interactions outside the community, may turn to each other for support and validation. Then there is a process of redefinition, in which the hate they experience in their lives is transformed into an affirmative solidarity. (Meekosha, 2002: 80)

Women with disabilities contend with the male gaze and also with how society sees them as disabled people (Ghai, 2002). Though denial of rights, lack of opportunity, and abuse are issues that have affected all women, these issues are compounded for women with disabilities by perceptions of them as passive, helpless, and asexual. These beliefs can put women with disabilities at risk of violence and abuse (de Silva de Alwis, 2009; Nixon, 2009). There are also issues that are more complex when accounting for a gendered disability perspective; issues such as prenatal testing, reproductive rights, sterilization, abortion, and the right to parent (Meekosha and Shuttleworth, 2009).

Trans people with disabilities are faced with the reality that disability can be used to delegitimize trans identity. Impairments can be used as a reason to gatekeep issues around trans identity or as a reason to not hold valid a person's identification as trans (Baril et al.,2020). Trans people with disabilities can be denied gender-affirming care due to disability, with many experiencing discrimination in health-care settings based on disability and gender identity. In fact, some LGBTQI2S people with disabilities experience abuse, such as verbal mistreatment, in health-care settings causing more people in the LGBTQI2S community to avoid seeking medical care. The traumatic effects of systemic oppression on people who identify as part of LGBTQI2S and disability communities can in turn impact disability, particularly by affecting mental health (Rodríguez-Roldán, 2020).

Violence against women, girls, and trans people with disabilities is best understood as the compound result of gender-based and disability-based violence. It results from patriarchal attitudes about women along with additional vulnerability that arises from having a disability. Some forms of violence against women with disabilities, including forced institutionalization and psychiatric interventions, are not as obvious because they are legal and socially accepted (INWWD, 2010).

## Empowered consciousness and social movement organizing

Not all people with disabilities experience the same oppression, but people with disabilities experience oppression in ways that are generalizable (Charlton, 1998). For Charlton, empowered consciousness involves a commitment to act. He says, 'There are many people with disabilities who have raised consciousness, but there are few who are politically active, who are committed to empowering others. These people are organizers, agitators, and educators who make up the disability rights movement' (1998: 16). As people are struggling against oppression, the very oppression against which people are struggling unites them and urges them to move forward in their exploration of self-identity.

In order for social movements to take shape, there must be a collective consciousness from which to work. It is not the only factor needed in social movement organizing, but it is an important and necessary one (Barnartt, 1996). The collective consciousness begins to emerge when people identify with a group and feel a sense of belonging to it. People may move into or out of the category of disability (Asch, 2001) and still others with impairments may not identify as having a disability (Barnes, 2003). That said, disability is a recognizable category and one that is necessary to name because 'it is impossible to fight the oppression of a group of people that does not exist' (Vehmas and Watson, 2014: 648).

Sharon Barnartt (1996) applies Klanderman's theory of collective consciousness formation to the disability community. There are three processes to consciousness formation. The first is consensus formation, where people with disabilities view personal troubles as shared with others. Rather than there being individual problems, people with disabilities identify as an oppressed group. People with disabilities emphasize the similarities among them rather than the differences which the medical community had long endorsed. The second process is consensus mobilization, where there is an attempt to create consensus among a population. This can be seen in the disability community through identification of collective issues such as employment, independent living, disability rights, and accommodations. The third process is action mobilization, which Barnartt (1996) identifies in the disability community as attempts to remedy collective issues like those above.

The disability rights movement is one born out of this process. The 1970s saw efforts by people with disabilities to increase their influence on matters affecting their own lives. A key advance came from a Rehabilitation International meeting in 1980 which was attended by several thousand participants who, for the most part, did not identify as having a disability. The organization, which is now the Council of Canadians with Disabilities, proposed an international disability led organization and, from this, Disabled Peoples' International (DPI) was founded in 1981. Human rights and non-discrimination were the foundational principles of the organization's work. Many DPI representatives became committee representatives for the International Year of the Disabled (IYD) in 1981, which Lindqvist (2015) flags as important because it involved an unprecedented level of participation by disabled people's organizations (DPOs) at the UN level. This led to important outcomes of the IYD: the World Programme of Action Concerning Disabled Persons and the International Decade of Disabled Persons, 1983–1992 (Lindqvist, 2015).

In 1984, Leandro Despouy was appointed as Special Rapporteur on Disability and Human Rights and reported to the Commission on Social Development. During the mid-term evaluation of the IYD, at a regional meeting in Slovenia, a recommendation made by two female delegates for a disability convention was turned down by the General Assembly. Follow-up requests were denied due to convention fatigue given the newly implemented Convention on the Elimination of Discrimination Against Women and the Convention on the Rights of the Child (Lindqvist, 2015).

Instead, the General Assembly issued the UN Standard Rules on the Equalization of Opportunities for People with Disabilities (the Standard Rules) (Quinn, 2011; United Nations, 2007). According to Stein (2007), the Standard Rules is the most significant soft law pertaining to people with disabilities. Importantly, the Standard Rules also furthered efforts toward disability being understood as a human rights issue (Lindqvist, 2015).

In 1992, the Special Rapporteur on Human Rights appointed a Disability Ombudsman, a High Commissioner for Human Rights was established the following year. While the Commission received a number of resolutions and recognized disability as a human rights issue (Lindqvist, 2015), in the decade that followed, thirteen of the seventeen disability-related complaints brought under various treaties were declared inadmissible because individual complaints were not permitted under those treaties (Stein, 2007). In 2000, UN High Commissioner for Human Rights, Mary Robinson, highlighted the importance of putting intellectual disabilities into a human rights context. In 2001, Robinson and the Special Rapporteur on Disability examined efforts to monitor and strengthen disability rights (Robinson, 2006).

Persistence within the disability movement kept the possibility of a convention on the agenda. The noticeable absence of people with disabilities from the 2000 Millennium Development Goals prompted Mexico to approach the UN General Assembly in 2001 (Kayess, 2011) with a request for a committee to investigate drafting a disability convention (Hoefmans and de Beco, 2010; McCallum, 2010).

The committee held eight sessions over five years with more than 100 people with disabilities and 70 DPOs present during the sessions (Kayess, 2011). Civil society and people with disabilities were given audience during the drafting process, something never before done in an international treaty process (Kayess, 2011; Hoefmans and de Beco, 2010; McCallum, 2010). An International Disability Caucus was established to cohesively represent civil society positions and, according to Quinn (2011), worked quite effectively. National human rights institutions also participated in the process. The United Nations CRPD was adopted in December 2006 and came into force in May 2008 (Quinn, 2011; United Nations, 2007). It is the first treaty since the Vienna Agreements and in terms of rights it offered 'an unprecedented level of protection' (United Nations, 2007: 9).

A unique feature of the monitoring provision of the CRPD is the involvement of people with disabilities in the monitoring process (Lindqvist, 2015). Internationally, a committee of independent experts is responsible for overseeing implementation by signatories who have ratified the CRPD. This is known as the Committee on the Rights of Persons with Disabilities and it works through dialogue between its expert members and the state making a submission. Over the years, Committees have seen an increase in non-governmental organization participation through submission of alternative reports which offer, as the name suggests, an alternative perspective to state reports (Lindqvist, 2015).

### Social movement organizing and women with disabilities

Here I discuss only women with disabilities because, at the time of my research, very little has surfaced about social movement organizing among trans people with disabilities; their experiences are not fully represented within existing movements. This is not to say that trans people are not a part of my research, they are.

Women with disabilities began consensus formation when they were exposing the ways in which the disability and women's movements, while each making the personal political (Nixon, 2009), were simultaneously excluding women with disabilities. As a group, women with disabilities also recognized that they had specific experiences that needed to be addressed. Often DPOs would send men to do advocacy work, but women began establishing networks to strengthen the voices of women with disabilities and bring attention to their specific experiences (Price, 2011).

My focus is on violence, so let me return to consensus formation, consensus mobilization, and action mobilization around gender and disability-based violence. Consensus formation is seen in the ways in which women with disabilities have come together to address gender-based violence in the disability community. This will be highlighted in many of the stories told in this book. Consensus mobilization was demonstrated within social movements when people first began to identify the lack of resources and accessible supports for women with disabilities experiencing violence. Action mobilization has been seen in the collective ways that women with disabilities have been working to address this lack of support and resources since the 1980s.

How does this affect identity formation which informs our self-awareness and consciousness? Identity formation is a process of people recognizing themselves, recognizing others, and being recognized by others in broad social groups. While the growth of feminism within the disability movement has had an impact on perceptions of disability, 'it has also been critically important to the development of individual and collective identities of disabled women' (Meekosha, 2002: 81).

One challenge in writing about oppression and consciousness is that the process is not linear. The causes and effects of identity formation and social movement organizing are complex. Collective identities can be produced by social movements and movements can also produce identities (Weldon, 2006). There is also the constant quest to support a broad movement while also supporting individuals in their efforts to understand their own self-identity in the process. This may create contradictions which are particularly complex for people with disabilities because of 'our isolation, stigmatization, and fragmentation into categories.' (Charlton, 1998: 154–155).

Where Barnartt (1996) describes collective consciousness formation in the disability community with three processes of consensus formation (which, as a reminder, is seeing experiences as shared), consensus mobilization (bringing together those with similar experiences), and action mobilization (collectively seeking solutions), Duncan developed a model that examined factors contributing to group consciousness and collective action. Why did some people in the women's movement transform their life experiences into activism? Her model accounted for personal and life experiences that influence group consciousness and collective action. She said that intrapersonal variables such as personal experience or personality contribute to group consciousness which then motivates collective action. In her theorization, group consciousness can give meaning to intrapersonal variables, thereby affecting collective action (Duncan, 1999: 613)

More specifically, Duncan found that feminist consciousness was related to higher levels of women's rights activism. If women were less likely to follow societal norms and more likely to see their experiences as political, they were more likely to engage in activism. Access to education was also marginally related to consciousness. The study showed that these relationships existed but did not address how they came to be (Duncan, 1999). Other research on violence-against-women activism has shown that heightened awareness about societal influences on domestic violence leads to increased activism and involvement with organizations working to end violence against women (Gill and Rehman, 2004).

I offer both models here because they each unpack the relationships between group consciousness and collective action. I want to build on this to uncover the specific kinds of conditions that challenge and also enable community organizers and advocates to do anti-gender-based violence work in the disability community. We turn now to the ways that social movement organizing among women with disabilities is unique. Once again, not much is yet known about inclusion of trans people with disabilities in these movements.

## What is unique about social movements of women with disabilities?

Nixon argues that divisions can happen within social movements and that,

> Those who experience compound oppressions are the most likely to experience negative effects as a result of the intersection of these oppressions. Women situated at the interface of disability and domestic violence usually have neither status nor resources to bring about social change. (2009: 85)

In the context of experiencing various forms of oppression, women with disabilities organize around issues that affect them. Price (2011) argues that for women with disabilities to organize and build a movement requires: 1) being able to identify both disability and gender as political issues as part of a consciousness-raising process; 2) having fully accessible movements that account for things like communication and spaces; 3) outreach and being able to make contact and engage in planning with other women with disabilities; and 4) addressing their exclusion from other movements.

Charlton (1998) speaks of the contradictions that may come between the individual and the collective and the necessity of a disability rights movement to unite the two. If individuals who have long been isolated politically, economically, and socially can find ways to connect to others who share common experiences, they will need to work to accommodate each other's differences. They need to do this in the context of a complicated history of fragmentation caused by putting people into categories.

Let me apply this specifically to movements led by women with disabilities. Resistance from men with disabilities to include issues affecting women with disabilities can be seen as working directly against disabled women's organizing. Similarly, the feminist movement has taken specific care to address embodiment and identity politics but has failed to address these for women with disabilities (Price, 2011). Feminists have engaged with difference, united by their efforts at empowerment and social equality, but have failed to engage women with disabilities. Ghai (2002) argues that this exclusion might be easier to fathom in the disability movement, which reflects the patriarchal character of society.

Historically, when feminists put women's experiences at the centre of research, they were unable to do so for disabled women because they lacked a frame of reference in which to centre and understand these experiences. This exclusion is the result of unquestioned social, psychological, and physical barriers, and a historical tendency for the feminist movement to fail to see disability as a political issue (Price, 2011). The women's movement may fight for the right to safe and legal abortions but when considering screening issues and decisions to abort, they may not see the complexity if the foetus has an impairment, for example. Furthermore, being excluded from both movements is more dangerous for women with disabilities experiencing violence because they have even more difficulty accessing support (Nixon, 2009). Meekosha argues that 'One dimension to the social transformation can be found in the degree to which women with disabilities feel more empowered to participate in society and able to use the social institutions to meet their economic, social, and cultural needs' (2002: 85). As noted earlier, there have been calls for a greater alliance between disability and trans studies (Baril et al., 2020; Slater and Liddiard, 2018). I could find limited resources on community organizing around gender-based violence that included trans people with disabilities even though it has been established that rates of disability in the trans community are high (Rodríguez-Roldán, 2020; Baril et al., 2020).

Enter then, the importance of documenting and researching on the experiences of women and trans people with disabilities. Disability studies has long called for the inclusion of lived experience in the research. This lived experience was needed for women with disabilities who were experiencing oppression. Morris (1991, 1993) worked to do just that: to expose lived experience, tell the stories of disabled women's oppression, and call on non-disabled women to be part of disabled women's empowerment.

> All oppressed groups need allies and, by doing research which gives voice to our experience, feminist researchers can help to empower disabled women. However, non-disabled feminists must also ask themselves where are the disabled researchers? students? academics? If they are truly to be allies we need them to recognize and challenge both direct and indirect discrimination. (Morris, 1993: 66)

Women with disabilities are unique in the challenges they face forming a collective. This is because of the historical exclusion from the two movements within which they should have been able to advance their concerns. They experienced a feminist movement that failed to understand disability issues as also political, and a disability movement which failed to fully appreciate their experience of disability as gendered. In fact, each movement excluded them in the very ways they have professed to experience exclusion themselves. In the face of resistance from those who should have been allies, women with disabilities have organized and worked to establish a movement that challenges mainstream notions of ability and gender while also working to resist their exclusion from feminist and disability movements.

Price (2011) argues that organizing by women with disabilities has been most difficult at the local level where isolation is most immediate and resources are not obvious or available. When women with disabilities have been able to contact other women with similar experiences, it contributes to self-confidence and consciousness-raising.

Advancing the disability rights agenda has served to help strengthen the disabled women's movement. The women's disability rights movement has advanced at national and international levels, yet women with disabilities struggle to establish the movement and keep it going (Price, 2011).

Meekosha (2002) offers three conditions that are necessary for social movement organizing among women with disabilities: 1) cultural and social dislocation – we have already established that women with disabilities experienced pressures of discrimination based on both gender and disability; 2) cultural expressions of experiences of discrimination – this can be seen in the way that women with disabilities have looked for commonalities and built support networks (I would add that this could include inside academia); and 3) symbolic challenges to the old way of doing things that reflect growing political awareness and movement solidarity. Women with disabilities and their organizations have sought action in the same way that non-disabled women have, but they also seek action on specific issues related to bodily invasion and family, domestic, and institutional violence. I end this section by emphasizing the importance of self-determination. Meyers, explains that

> Self-determination … is best understood as an ongoing process of exercising a repertoire of agentic skills — skills that enable individuals to construct their own self-portraits and self-narratives and that thereby enable them to take charge of their lives. Construing self-determination this way demonstrates women's need for expanded agency, for it discloses how patriarchal cultures illegitimately interfere with women's agentic skills. (2002: 3)

Women with disabilities face unique challenges to realizing their right to self-determination, a factor which is necessary for living a life free of violence.

## Conclusion

Some common threads run through the theories examined in this chapter. Colonial, capitalist, patriarchal systems could not exist without oppression, specifically women's oppression. Marxist, antiracist, Indigenous, disability, feminist, and legal critical theories make visible the complexities that emerge when the female subject is not an able-bodied, white, middle-class woman. They also recognize that identity cannot be separated into the parts which comprise it. While scholars generally agree that categories of identities are constructed, they differ to some extent in their treatment and understanding of this construction. What is clear is that oppression based on being a woman with a disability is internalized. Feminist disability scholars theorize that disability is part of an identity that is socially constructed; however, there are differences around the ways and extent to which society is responsible for disablement and oppression.

Given the prevalence of poverty and oppression among women and trans people with disabilities, application of these theories is necessary.

Rather than claim that there are gaps in theoretical knowledge on how to unpack, understand, and mitigate oppression, I posit that there are gaps in the extension of knowledge to women and trans people with disabilities experiencing violence. By starting from an intersectionality perspective, theorizations on gender and disability oppression encompass the complexities of identity. While there are some common threads, the manifestation and implementation of oppression is understood to be influenced by the composition of one's identity. Solutions can only be found outside the colonial, capitalist, patriarchal system that has survived by oppressing those that it has Othered.

While Charlton (1998) concludes that disability oppression is here to stay, he believes there are two factors to consider: the capacity of oppressive systems to reproduce themselves, and that oppression also generates resistance, empowerment, and, hopefully, from that liberation and freedom. I want to draw on this insight and apply it to gender-based violence. I too believe that individual resistance contributes to the collective, and that insights into why and how activists and advocates do their work will contribute to our understanding of resisting gender-based violence in the disability community.

## Notes

1.  Importantly, research on violence against trans people with disabilities is limited. However, research on gender-based violence will often note people with disabilities and trans and non-binary people as separate categories of people affected by violence, but not as a group in and of itself (see, for example, United Nations Population Fund, 2018b).
2.  The first cases of coronavirus were detected in December 2019, but a global health pandemic was not declared until March 2020. Because the virus is contagious with potentially severe health impacts, countries restricted travel, individuals were asked to stay at home, and states of emergency were enacted globally (see World Health Organization, 2019).

# CHAPTER 3
# Methodology

My research methodology is rooted in Freire's (1970) work which argues that only when the oppressed perceive their situation as oppressive and reflect on their situation with a view towards changing it, can they be liberated from their oppression. According to Freire, knowledge cannot be imposed upon people. Rather, emphasis must be on dialogue and cooperation in moving toward action. This is an important consideration in my work.

Ayesha Vernon writes about doing research with disabled Black women as a disabled Black woman herself. She describes her research being as much about her own experience as it is about others. She recognizes that

> the closer our subject matter to our own life and experience the more we can expect our own beliefs about the world to enter into and shape our work, to influence the very questions we pose and the interpretations we generate from our findings (1997: 158).

Like Vernon, I am in control as the researcher and I am also inserted into the research as both researcher and subject. This requires recognition of my bias rather than avoidance of it. In considering whether my research is exploitative or if it is emancipatory, I follow Vernon's description of her efforts to ensure her research was emancipatory.

> Other principles of emancipatory research include socialising rather than individualising. For example, locating the causes of their 'problems' in the structures of an oppressive society rather than blaming the individual (Oliver, 1992). This was done in a variety of ways: by a careful phrasing of the questions asked in the interview, by sharing my own experiences (where relevant) so that they felt they were not alone in what they had experienced. And, finally, in collectivising their experiences through an in-depth analysis of the data and disseminating this information both to the women in the study and to the wider community through written publications (e.g. Vernon, 1996a) (1997: 162–163).

This book focuses not on individual experiences of violence, but rather on experiences of working to end violence. I asked questions that explored challenges and hopes around doing advocacy work. At times, if I felt it was relevant, I shared my experience doing research. I also began my interviews with an explanation of why I am researching in this area. This required that I share information about my own lived experiences.

My research reaches across cultures, countries, and contexts to uncover some commonalities in the work done to address gender-based violence against people with disabilities. It may be viewed as methodologically challenging to account for cross-context differences in types of oppression, and the work done in resistance to it. In thinking through this challenge, I am drawn back to Jenny Morris. She cites a defence made by a feminist writer who excluded disability from feminist analysis on the basis of cross-cultural differences that could not be accounted for. The author argued that oppression can take different forms in different cultures, therefore it is difficult to generalize. Morris' rebuttal bears repeating here:

> These are really flimsy arguments. Racism also takes different forms in different cultures; yet recent feminist analysis has, quite rightly, argued that Black women's experiences and interests must be placed at the heart of feminist research and theory. Ramazangolu's second statement is an extraordinary denial of the socio-economic base of the oppression which older people and disabled people experience (1991).

It is not the experiences of oppression that are central to my analysis – although they are important and they do come up from time to time – rather it is the experience of resisting this oppression that is critical to my research. While there may be differences in contexts that influence one's ability to resist, the similarities – which I expected to find – are a strong point to draw upon in analysis.

## Methods

After obtaining ethics approval from York University, participants were recruited by networking with organizations in Canada and internationally. I reached out to my networks via e-mail, Twitter, Instagram, and Facebook. I also joined disability studies groups on Facebook and requested permission to post my call for participants. Snowballing was also used as a recruitment method. When people within my networks responded, many offered or agreed to share my call for participants with their networks. After an interview concluded, I asked the participant to send information about my research to anyone they thought might be interested. I endeavoured to reach participants globally who encompassed a wide range of backgrounds, geographic locations, and identities.

Semi-structured, face-to-face, and virtual interviews were conducted with advocates, service providers, and community organizers who work specifically with women with disabilities who have experienced violence, or who work with organizations that work to resist gender-based violence against people with disabilities. According to Walliman (2006) and Bernard (2013), semi-structured interviews combine structured questions with a flexible structure to allow the asking of open-ended questions.

Furthermore, doing face-to-face or video interviews where possible allowed me to gauge the depth of the answers and to confirm the question was understood in order to ensure quality answers (Walliman, 2006). It also allowed me to probe for additional information where needed (Bernard, 2013; Czaja and Blair, 2005). In instances where I could not meet the participant in person, I used Zoom to record the interviews. Audio from the interview was saved and transcribed. Concerns around and benefits of using videoconferencing for interviews have been identified in the literature, particularly ethical concerns related to using third-party software such as Zoom which maintains the right to record conversations (Lo Iacono et al., 2016; Sullivan, 2012). I felt that using the software offered through my university would help to mitigate this concern. While it has been noted that technical issues might interrupt the flow of the interview and the potential that interviewees may not open up as much over technology as they would face-to-face (Lo Iacono et al., 2016; Janghorban et al., 2014; Sullivan, 2012), this was rare and technical issues seemed to strengthen the resolve of the participants to communicate their responses. Some studies have found that participants may open up more if they are in a comfortable and convenient environment and use of videoconferencing also has the benefit of reaching participants who may not be able to meet face-to-face (Lo Iacono et al., 2016; Janghorban et al., 2014; Sullivan, 2012).

The goal of the interviews was to document community organizer and advocate experiences working with women with disabilities who have been subjected to violence. Fourteen individual interviews were conducted and, in the end, only thirteen were used. These interviews addressed challenges, motivations, and hopes of advocates and community organizers.

## The participants

I did all interviews in person, on the phone or through a video call. I sent the transcripts to the participants for review. Five participants were interviewed at an agreed-upon location in Toronto (one participant was visiting from another city). One interview was done in a van while travelling between meetings in Hyderabad, India at the request of the participant. I began one interview face-to-face in Katmandu, Nepal, with the second half done virtually due to interruptions in Nepal. Three interviews, with participants in Australia, Bangladesh, and the United States, were done via Zoom. One interview with a participant in Toronto was done over the phone using a recorder. Two interviews were done using WhatsApp and a recorder at the request of the interviewees in Kenya (though one participant was from and working in Ghana). One interview was done via e-mail because the interviewee was more confident writing than speaking in English. As a precaution, I contacted the ethics committee representative and confirmed that using alternative technology to that which was noted in my ethics proposal was permitted.

Nine countries are represented in this study. In terms of disability representation, seven participants identified physical disabilities, one participant was blind, three identified interacting with the psychiatric system, one identified a learning disability, and it should be noted that some identified multiple disabilities or did not name their disability experience. Noticeably absent were folk from the Deaf community and people with intellectual disabilities.

## Participant profiles

*Amal* is a woman with a physical disability from Yemen who has worked with women with disabilities since 2000. She promotes the inclusion of women with disabilities in sports. Amal also helped to establish a society for women with disabilities which supports rural women to complete their studies so they can attend university.

*Fran* has been doing community activism work in women's and disability movements in Toronto for about 25 years. She began working on gender-based violence and disability following the completion of her master's degree. Fran has worked on issues ranging from support services to intimate partner, caregiver, and family violence. She has worked throughout her career to create more gender- and disability-inclusive movements.

*Keegan* is a community activist in Toronto who does work around disability and violence, consent, and sexual assault. They have been doing this work for five to seven years. They are actively involved in anti-violence marches and protests in their community.

*Patricia* is an art therapist, a trained social worker, and a graduate student from Toronto. She has been working in the area of women's mental health since 2010. She worked in supportive housing directly alongside people, or on their behalf. This involved advocating for things like housing and income support, or providing support during landlord disputes. As an art therapist, she has done expressive art with various groups across Toronto. She is currently completing her PhD.

*Karen* has been doing voluntary advocacy work in the disability sector in Australia since 2013, but her work with people with disabilities goes back to 1993 when she worked with children with disabilities as an early-childhood educator. Karen worked as a front-line manager for an autistic day programme but lost her job after filing a complaint with the Disability Commissioner about abusive practices at the centre where she worked. She is a trainer and assessor for people entering support roles in the disability sector.

*Elizabeth* is a trained teacher who specializes in adolescent reproductive health. She is a programme manager with the Ghana Blind Union, coordinating advocacy efforts for blind and partially sighted persons. She focuses on issues of education, health, and employment. She has been doing disability advocacy work for 12 years.

*Sarah* is a 21-year-old university student in the United States who has been doing disability advocacy since she was 12 years old, and anti-violence work since she was about 16. Much of her advocacy efforts are in supporting survivors and raising awareness on her university campus about sexual violence. She brings a disability lens to her advocacy efforts and works as a victim-support specialist at her school. Outside of school, Sarah is involved in advocating for disability issues at the federal level, particularly around psychiatric interventions. She is currently completing a degree in disability studies in the United States.

*Usha* is a retired schoolteacher from India who worked at a school for blind and partially sighted children. As a blind woman herself, Usha has worked for 20 years with communities and families to raise awareness about the importance of education. She focused her efforts on taking children out of difficult and often violent situations in rural villages and getting them into school. Coming from a royal family, she often paid the school fees for students and bought a house where young women could live while they were in college or university and until they found a job.

*Charlie* is a social worker in Toronto who works with primarily female-identified adults with mental health and substance-abuse challenges. They have worked primarily as a front-line counsellor and case manager. They help folks who have often experienced trauma navigate support, health care, and psychiatric care systems. Recognizing the complexities of gender identity and disability, Charlie prioritizes being inclusive and supportive to the folks they work with.

*Molly* is a 23-year-old university student in Manitoba who has worked to raise awareness about sexuality and disability. She has done self-advocacy around her own experience related to gender-based violence and disability. She has also done awareness raising about consent culture on university campuses. She has worked on gender-based violence in the disability community for four years.

*Jane* is the executive director of an organization for women with disabilities in Kenya. As a woman with a physical disability, she has been doing advocacy and awareness raising about issues affecting women with disabilities since 2014. Jane and her organization offer programmes on the elimination of violence against women with disabilities, access to justice, and rights awareness.

*Tika* had polio as a young child and has been doing advocacy, lobbying, disability rights, and gender equality promotion in Nepal since 1998. She started an association of women with disabilities that works on discrimination, empowerment, capacity building, human rights, and justice issues. The association's efforts have seen the establishment of 16 organizations of women with disabilities across the country.

*Misti* is woman with a physical disability in Bangladesh who has been doing advocacy work on gender-based violence and disability since 2007. She is also the founder and director of an organization for women with disabilities in her country. Her organization raises awareness to stop violence against women with disabilities and to disseminate information on how to get access to justice. These are critical concerns for women and girls with disabilities in Bangladesh, and their families.

## Analysis

The data was analysed using an objectivist grounded theory framework, which is a type of text analysis that values a systematic approach to generating a theory from the data. Rather than starting with a specific hypothesis, this method allows for a theory to emerge from a close reading of the texts. The specific method involves coding the text for themes and generating a theory from the themes (Strauss and Corbin, 1994). Stemler (2001) tells us that content analysis is useful for examining trends or patterns. It seeks to take large amounts of text and break it down into fewer categories (Weber, 1990).

I initially attempted to use Nvivo to code the interviews but, after coding two interviews in this way, coding for themes felt forced and I decided that Nvivo would be better used once I had the codes I needed. Instead, I read each interview and noted themes as they emerged.

Several ideas were repeated in the interviews, making it easier to find the themes manually. Each time a new theme emerged, I read through previously coded interviews to ensure that the new theme had not been missed. I did this until all the interviews were done and all of the themes documented. I then began to look for relationships among the themes. It became clear that the themes centred on experiences of oppression and transformations.

Once the themes had been identified and written up, I returned to Nvivo and coded the interviews using the software to cross-check my manual findings. I reread the transcripts after writing up my findings with a better understanding of the interviews as a collection, and I was able to code in more detail. I decided to use the themes that were identified in six or more of the interviews as this number essentially represented half of the sample.

I also decided to tell the stories of all 13 participants. I felt I could not simply separate their stories into their parts without also identifying how the parts were connected. Each participant, while contributing to an overall understanding of the themes, had a story that needed to also be told in its entirety. I have made an intentional effort to draw extensively on the participant's own words in order to give context to participant experiences.

Gorman (2007) argues that a feminist dialectal materialistic approach to understanding data emerges from interviews. This allows us to analyse what is being said in a highly contextualized way. She frames interviews as dialogue and testimony for the participants in her study on individual and collective struggle. She makes the case that what we include serves to contextualize what is being said beyond coded analysis.

Occasionally, I use longer quotes within the stories and findings. This is done intentionally in order to honour the testimony of my participants. Sometimes, when asked about an aspect of the work, a participant gave long answers which I think speaks to the depth of knowledge and work done by participants. For example, if a participant gave me a detailed list of the things that needed to be done to establish an organization or organize within a community, I could approach the information in two ways: I could summarize what the participant said and relate it to my findings, or I could include the response as it was given in order to emphasize the lengths to which participants needed to go in doing their work. I was concerned that if I summarized the work, these important details would not be documented and I did not want them to be forgotten. In addition to contextualizing the answers, my strategy serves to document the important details that sometimes get lost in analysis.

I sent all transcripts and stories to participants to ensure that I had captured their experiences as they had wished. I worked with each participant to make changes as necessary, and all stories have been approved. It should also be noted that two of the participants have remarked to me that I captured their stories well. One participant indicated that this is the first time she has told her story in such detail to anyone and that she was happy with the outcome. This reaffirmed that my decision to tell participant stories was the right one.

The number of themes aligned with the number of stories, so I decided to tell a story to introduce each of the themes. I ran a query in Nvivo to determine which themes were strongest in each interview and which interviews most strongly reflected each theme. I compared the frequencies of each and assigned stories to themes as far as was possible. Some interviews strongly represented more than one theme and some themes were strongly represented in more than one interview. I used my judgement where needed and explained my decisions throughout. I then cross-checked to ensure the quotes from the stories did not overlap with the quotes used in the overall analysis of each theme. In cases where I have used portions of quotes on more than one occasion, this is intentional.

# CHAPTER 4
# Participant experiences

Before I discuss experiences of doing advocacy work for the participants in the study, I want to briefly outline the points they raised in terms of the types of issues people with disabilities still face. This is not the primary focus of this book, but it does provide the context within which the participants are working. Two of the participants, one in Canada and one in the United States, directly mention the rise in hate crimes against people with disabilities. Other types of violence discussed have been forced institutionalization; violent treatment in the name of psychiatric care; sexual violence perpetrated by various individuals, including care workers; and violence perpetrated by family members or intimate partners. Violence has not been limited to one or two domains. Participants experienced or addressed violence in the community, family, workplace, university, or institutionally. Some of these instances will be discussed in the following chapters.

Common experiences discussed by participants were negative perceptions of disability, lack of representation in disability and feminist movements, inadequately addressing the intersecting nature of our identities and oppressions, structural violence, rights issues, challenges accessing justice, and lack of policy and government commitment. Sometimes these issues were identified when I asked what challenges the participants faced, and sometimes they were identified as motivations when I asked participants how or why they began to do their work.

## Negative perceptions about disability

### Amal – Yemen

I reached out to Amal through my social networks. We had met previously at an event focused on women with disabilities organized by Mobility International in Eugene, Oregon. Amal requested to be interviewed via e-mail so I sent her the questions. She responded and I followed up.

Amal is a woman with a physical disability. For nine years she has worked in the areas of public relations, rehabilitation, training, and as media officer for an association for women with disabilities in Yemen. She is currently Assistant Secretary-General of the Yemeni Paralympic Committee and Assistant Secretary-General of the General Federation for the Sports of Persons with Disabilities, a sports centre established for women with disabilities.

Some of Amal's work has included raising awareness about the effects of war on women with disabilities. She works on these issues because of the prevalence of violence against women with disabilities. She has been working on disability rights since 2000 and started this work because, as was her own case, most women with disabilities are isolated in their homes and experience negative reactions from society.

She left her home despite traditional beliefs that it is a disgrace for women to do so. She says that, though people looked at her differently because of her disability, she persisted and left home to get an education. After completing her studies, Amal worked with an organization for women with disabilities. In addition to pursing her own education, promoting education for other women and girls with disabilities is important to Amal. She participated in the establishment of an association to help rural women with disabilities finish their studies and go to university.

When I ask Amal about the rewards of doing her work, she says it is rewarding to see large numbers of women with disabilities become involved in society. She feels that it is important that women are able to participate in sports regardless of societal perceptions. She ends by telling me that her goal is being reached, and some people in her society are becoming aware of the importance of the rights of women with disabilities.

### Negative perceptions

Amal raises the cultural beliefs and attitudes that impact inclusion for women with disabilities in her country. The impact of negative perceptions of disability was raised by eleven participants. One participant describes having an invisible disability and the perceptions she has experienced:

> I was diagnosed very early. I knew about it. I grew up with it. It formed part of my identity. But the other thing is there was nothing that I could show people that I had a disability. So, it was very frustrating because of all the things that dyslexic people get told throughout their life: that they should just try harder, they shouldn't be so day dreamy.

Sometimes these perceptions are felt when the participants are out in the community and, perhaps, the disability is more visible. One woman describes going to school when she was younger and being told by people that because she was disabled, she could not do anything. She recounts various experiences over the years of being discriminated against, isolated, and harassed because she is a woman with a disability. Other participants also describe negative perceptions they are subject to from community members, specifically because they are women with disabilities. Usha, who worked with communities in India to get more blind and visually impaired girls into school, describes several stories that indicate these perceptions exist. She tells me about one father who is unable to accept a child because of her disability and so he leaves:

> [The] father goes and leaves child because [the mother] gave birth to a visually impaired child. He just leaves her and goes and gets married somewhere and the mother has to take care of the child. She brought

like that, one lady. She was a beautiful looking lady ... she had a girl, cute thing she was. She just brought her and put her at my feet saying, 'Please may you take care of her. My husband left me because I gave birth to this child.' Yeah, there are so many stories like that.

The women describe being perceived as unable to be involved in romantic relationships or unable to have a family. Usha, being unmarried, will often counsel young women with disabilities telling them that they will be okay if they do not get married. Other times, if the women are married and then acquire a disability, their families do not respond well. One participant tells me that, in Ghana.

Those women who lose their sight at the point in time in their lives, especially those who are semi-literate, when it happens like that you see their husbands or spouses taking advantage of them ... We have some specific situations where they even deny them their own children. They just take the children away from them and just classify them as being sick.

Negative perceptions of women with disabilities span cultures and contexts. As we will see in the next story, Fran describes growing up in Ontario facing negative perceptions from others in her community about women with disabilities. Specifically, perceptions that women with disabilities are incapable of relationships. A participant in Kenya describes growing up with similar perceptions. She says, 'I was never accepted fully in the community because when it comes to issues of marriage, relationships, no one wants to get a woman with disability. Nobody wants to marry a woman with a disability.' The same participant describes persistent negative perceptions as an ongoing challenge to her advocacy work: 'The challenge is that people's perception still, around disability, they have not changed. And the change I wanted is something that takes time.'

Some of the participants speak about how negative perceptions of disability made them feel. One participant discusses feeling disheartened when being interviewed for a job and her ability to do the job being questioned based on her personal care management. Another racialized participant tells me about shame. She says, 'It's the shame that is created from treatment or being hospitalized and being told that I'm a dysfunctional person from a dysfunctional family. And I'm always going to be that way. And so I need to think differently and cope and be a different person and be like every white person.'

Another participant expresses anger about negative perceptions of disability. She feels that 'It's okay to be angry and I think all too often we can't be angry because we're infantilised or hyper-medicalized and psychiatrized – it's not a word, but it's fine.' Negative perceptions around psychiatric care came up in other ways as well. One participant describes a meeting with a government official about policies to increase beds in institutions with the rationale of helping to protect families from violent behaviour. The psychiatric system is defended as a means of protecting people from violent patients.

Negative perceptions were expressed about physical, sensory, and psychiatric disabilities. They were also expressed in terms of how disability interacted with gender. These perceptions cannot be separated because they are experienced at the same time.

## Lack of representation in movements

### Fran – Toronto, Canada

Fran has been an activist in the women's movement and in the disability community for about 25 years. She began her work after finishing a master's degree and taking up a research position with DAWN Canada, researching violence against women with disabilities. She was looking at access to services for women with disabilities who experienced intimate partner violence, caregiver violence, and violence from other family members. Like several of the other participants who describe their own experience as part of their work, or reflected within it, Fran tells me:

> It was doing that work when I came to see my own experience. And I hadn't really been out about it, and it took me a very long time to kind of be, you know, sort of, out about my own experience but was certainly seeing the difficulties that women were experiencing being able: 1) to get out; 2) to be able to stay out; and 3) to get, you know, access to services to support them in their healing. It just kind of was such a heart breaking and really frustrating and I know that also during that time – I'm trying to make the links ... that I was also trying to find services in my own recognition of violence in my own relationship and really struggled. So, I could see a lot of parallels around what other women were talking about and also my own experience.

As her activism progressed, Fran found herself frustrated with the lack of representation of disabled women in work on gender-based violence. In the same way as other participants, the absence of women in the movement in the early days surfaces as a motivation for Fran. Fran shares her feelings about this:

> I found it really frustrating. Really frustrating. And I'm not sure that that has really changed. I think more disabled women are taking this on and doing work and I really would love to see more disabled women doing the work at the policy level. Cathy MacPherson was doing work within government looking at violence against people with disabilities. It wasn't a gendered lens but certainly she was bringing it to the table in her work as a policy analyst. And I learned a lot from her as well. Pat Israel also, one of the founding women with the DisAbled Women's Network Canada. You know, bringing those issues to the forefront but definitely I was, probably, one of maybe two other women with visible disabilities who were at the table. I suspect, Tammy, there were lots of

women with disabilities at the table but who were not making those connections.

Fran talks about the challenge of integrating women's experience into the disability movement and the belief by many men doing disability activism in the early days of her work that including gender and women's issues would weaken the movement. She explains:

> You know, I remember having arguments, not arguments but real disagreements, with disability activists. Many of them who were men who really felt like talking about disability and gender was going to split the movement; was going to really take away from the efforts that many in the disability rights movement were working hard to bring to the forefront. And then to add another layer which is looking at gender, which is looking at race, which is looking at sexuality, was gonna splinter the movement.

> And so that has been one of the reasons why the DisAbled Women's Network did form is because the women's movement was predominantly a non-disabled white woman's movement. They weren't really recognizing that disabled women were women. And recognizing that we too also face issues around inequities related to employment, education, and all the rest of it. But, you know, as well there is the violence against disabled women and then, in the disability rights movement, were men with disabilities who are also at risk. So, you know, to have those conversations is challenging at the best of times.

Interestingly, Fran sees those doing gender-based violence work as more receptive to including women with disabilities than those from the disability community. She attributes this, to some extent, to funding priorities:

> I feel like there's been more take up from the people that are doing the work around gender-based violence than within the disability community. And I would say that even more now because I feel like funding has really changed as far as programming. I don't know of any disability organizations that are doing gender-specific programming; the Centre for Independent Living, they weren't really looking at that for a very long time, not even violence workshops for women. Only because then there would be this uproar from men: 'What about us?' You know, the Anne Johnson Health Station, for a very long time they worked around creating gender-specific workshops on a variety of issues. But that was really because there was someone within the organization that fought very hard ... saw it really as a priority. And, so, efforts were made to have all kinds of workshops and support groups and whatever for women. And then that stopped. So, I don't often see very many organizations that are disability focused or led by folks with disabilities that are taking a gendered lens.

She tells me that sometimes disability gets raised by non-disabled people, even now, but it's complicated:

> But it's not their issue. I think it feels complicated to be raising the issue while there is also someone from the community at the table but, you know, I don't want to be the only spokesperson. Right. I'm not the spokesperson for disabled women and gender-based violence. I don't think this is my issue only. But I think that, quite frankly, non-disabled women who are also marginalized because of race or sexuality should be able to know that I would also raise those issues at the table when they're not there. But I don't feel quite as confident that my – that issues of disabled women – will be raised if there isn't somebody there.

There is an interesting point here. People may feel awkward raising disability if there is someone with a disability at the table, yet Fran would raise other aspects of identity as a disabled woman at the table. The challenge being that there are so few women with disabilities addressing violence, that one easily becomes the spokesperson, the one expected to raise the issue. Fran is clear that she does not want to be the only one doing this work.

Like many of the participants I interviewed, Fran raises the importance of government priorities in addressing gender-based violence in the disability community. In many ways, accessing funding for services is a challenge even if the government knows there are concerns. When I ask her what keeps her going, she discusses the need to keep fighting for support for shelters and other services to be accessible:

> I feel like the good fight's not over. I do feel like we've made progress. There's been, not now with this current government, but I think that there are folks in government that are really trying to make sure that there is a funding pocket available. Certainly, there was a time, maybe five years ago, when the Ministry of Community and Social Services, it's changed its name, but certainly they were seeing the need to support front-line shelters, and transitional houses, to really start looking at making them more accessible. But the capital costs of making a shelter really accessible is quite high. So, you've got a lot of these shelters that are located in older houses that really can't be retrofitted unless they go to a brand-new location, and a lot of the shelters just don't have capital campaigns going as yet to be able to look at that.

She feels that violence against women is not a government priority. People working in shelters have to do what they can to even keep them going, let alone make them accessible:

> You know, they're probably seeing more and more women coming in through their door, where they're just having to make do in order to keep her safe. But it it's not an ideal situation and, you know, those same shelters are now facing huge cuts with this provincial government. Violence against women is not a priority. It has not really been a priority

for many, many years. Even though people are aware of the issues, I feel like just being able to keep their doors open is really a priority for lots of shelters.

I wanted to know if doing this work is at all related to self-perception or consciousness among my study participants. So, I ask Fran if her self-perception has changed over time. She tells me:

> That's a great question. I would say yes, definitely. I think probably, Tammy, for me in the very beginning stages of thinking about this and my own experience. You know, I grew up like many of us did, in a culture that doesn't see folks with disabilities being in relationships, don't see us as viable partners or, when people are in relationships, that it's mired in all kinds of other stuff, right? I mean perception wise. I've done lots of work around sexuality and relationships, that I think for me, in the earlier days it was like I don't ever believe that I was to blame for this. But I think that I really battle disrupting the narrative around disability and relationships in my own sort of coming out around the issue.

Like many women with disabilities, Fran alludes to internalizing the negative perceptions of women with disabilities perpetuated in society. She goes on to tell me:

> Yeah, so I think I had my own internalized ableism, my own internalized perceptions. I think I really did not want to contribute by coming out around my experience of violence, to the beliefs and stereotypes that were out there about people with disabilities and, in particular, women with disabilities and our perceived vulnerabilities.

She raises the important point that sometimes the service providers can also be survivors of violence, but we do not often think about how many women get into this work because of their own experiences with violence:

> You know, certainly in the last, I would say, ten years, when we think about doing work with survivors, we typically have framed people who are survivors as being someone different than service providers. Right? So, we have to make sure we have survivors at the table and, you know, we have to listen to survivors … there are survivors who are already here at the table, who are also providers of services and supports. I think, I mean, not all of us, absolutely not, but I think there are many of us that get into this work because of our own experience. But, when we do a call out for survivors, we don't often see the duality of workers' experiences: they may also be survivors.

Fran raises the importance of education, but in a different context to that highlighted by other participants in the study. While many participants discussed the importance of getting their own education and helping other young girls access education as a form of empowerment, Fran discusses structural issues within the education system, addressing issues of disability at a post-secondary level. Specifically, she mentions that university programmes are not good at including gender in disability studies or adequately including disability in women and gender studies programmes. She says, 'I know that we need to be looking at this work through an anti-oppressive lens, but I think that we need to really carve out space for marginalized folks within our own community to have access to this material, and resources, and scholarship.' There are also issues of who has access to what level of education and where the opportunities lie:

> I think there can be some amazing work at the college level and students coming out of college that are interested in this but seeing that they can't really go anywhere with one course. That they have to go on and do a disability studies degree, which isn't always going to be possible for everybody.

About the future of the movement, Fran is cautiously optimistic. She is honest in telling me that what keeps her hopeful is the possibility of getting to a point where violence against women, including disabled women, and misogyny are not tolerated and is also cautiously optimistic about the future:

> I don't at all have an answer because it's definitely something that I think about a lot. I don't want to do this for the rest of my life. I do want to see younger women taking this up. And I wonder how do we pass the torch? Interestingly enough, I think there are a lot of younger folks, and when I say 'women' I mean non-binary folks, who are doing work, awesome work, around social justice and disability but who do not see this as a priority.

Fran's work spans more than two decades. She has shown dedication to the movement as an advocate for eradicating violence against women with disabilities. Like many participants doing this work, her experience gives us insight into challenges of representation, structural barriers, and competing priorities. What Fran's story also gives us is insight into why advocates persist within these contexts, among the reasons being wanting a better situation for others and a hope that others will continue with the movement.

### Representation in the disability movement

Fran's story reflects many of the themes that emerged in my interviews. It also reflects what we already know about the history of gender and disability within various movements. I will start first by addressing what participants said about representation in the disability movement, then move on to women's movements. Fran's story speaks to the historical absence of women with disabilities in both movements in that she was often the only voice in the spaces she entered during her work in Ontario. Misti in Bangladesh expresses her motivations for starting an organization of women with disabilities as being because men dominated the disability movement in her country. She describes how, when they started the women's organization, the reaction from men with disabilities was that they should lead their organization, but the women resisted:

Tika, who also started a disability organization for women, in Nepal, faced similar circumstances with only a few women involved in the disability movement at the time she joined. Additionally, she describes instances where men were organizing training sessions in the disability sector but women with disabilities were not being addressed or asked to participate. Later, when we talk about community organizing, we will see what Tika did to address this gap.

Sarah is in the United States. She describes her understanding of the history of the disability movement before she became involved, and compares the movement now to a time when the disability movement was primarily led by white, physically disabled men. She also highlights the divergent ways that violence in the disability community is discussed:

> We're kind of in a new wave of disability advocacy and it's called disability justice which began in 2006 and it was a wave started by queer, disabled, women of colour. So, these were people who were so focused on, kind of, looking at these intersecting identities, and uplifting voices that have been silent in the disability community for a long time. And a lot of them talk a lot about violence and have talked a lot about hate crimes because that's something that our community has definitely focused a lot more on because we're so vulnerable to hate crimes. And a lot of times, these hate crimes come in the form of gender violence ... we have a lot of disabled women and disabled non-binary people who are talking about this a lot more.

> So, I definitely think that it's all because of leadership change. Because, before, our leaders were, you know, white physically disabled men and now our leaders are very, very diverse and a lot of them are artists, which I think is really cool ... violence is a really hard thing to talk about. Having artists at our leadership, they're less scared to talk about the hard topics; where I feel like, before, we were always trying to talk about something that was politically strategic.

Like Sarah, Molly in Winnipeg talks about historical domination of the disability movement by men who did not allow space for women or younger people to get involved:

> In Winnipeg, the disability community is very small and people often talk about Winnipeg as the centre of disability advocacy because in the seventies we were. But it's the same people clinging on. It's a lot of men seizing these roles and never allowing space for women or, especially, gender non-conforming folks and so then it's just like not allowing

younger people to get involved in the conversation and they're not ready to give up their space.

While Sarah and Molly discuss the historical absence of women and gender non-conforming people generally, Charlie, who works with women with substance abuse and mental health disabilities, also talks about their motivation to be involved in advocating with and for women because they never felt like their own identity was represented. She says, 'That felt like a reason to commit myself to, to working with my people.'

Karen in Australia talks about men continuing to represent the disability movement publicly even today:

> When it comes to media, or exposure in the media, or the people who are being put forward in the disability community as spokespeople for the general public, they're still men. So, it's still men in a wheelchair or men who have children with a disability. You know, there's kind of a level or line that women get where they're respected for the work that they do. Then when we take it to the next level of work or presenting information to mainstream media, it's often men who are represented over women, which is a shame because it's the women with disabilities that are doing a lot of the groundwork.

The disability movement has historically been dominated by men and community organizers in this study speak about the continued domination of the movement by men. This motivates many of the participants to do their work and to contribute to representation which, as we see in the next chapter, comes with raised awareness, advancement of advocacy and rights issues, and enhanced community organizing.

### Representation in women's movements

Jane in Kenya tells me that the reason she started an organization of women with disabilities is because of the lack of representation of disability in the women's movements in her country. Tika, in Nepal, also indicated that when she approached women's movements to include women with disabilities, she was commonly met with the response that this was not their responsibility or that they did not have the resources or accessible spaces to include women with disabilities in their activities. This lack of representation is evident when we think about who is invited to the table. This is also seen in Fran's story when she describes often being the only woman with a disability at the table and the feeling of not wanting to be the only one doing the work, or being the only one expected to represent the experiences of women with disabilities.

Molly in Winnipeg explains that there are several communities where disability is excluded. She describes the feelings that this creates for her: 'It's also hard to have all these communities that really rally together but then just leave out the disabled voices. I think it is really isolating.' She also describes her surprise when she was invited to speak on a panel about sexual violence as a woman with a disability. She says:

> I was invited to speak on a panel about sexual violence and, as a disabled person, I was like 'Oh my god! You're finally including us in the conversation.' And just having those moments where people [say], 'You also deserve a seat here and this also impacts you,' has been really rewarding.

Sarah, in the United States, also describes her work to raise awareness about disability in anti-violence campaigns on campus, and her continuous efforts to raise disability issues. She does this because, as she explains, disability played a part in her victimization so it is important to her to address it. Like the disability movement, women's movements are still slow to catch up. Participants often tried advocating or organizing through one of these movements only to be met with the same resistance from both. So having more than one avenue through which to advocate simply meant more barriers to achieving inclusion. Perhaps this is why multiple women started their own organizations specifically for and with women with disabilities.

## Inadequately addressing intersectionality

### Keegan – Toronto, Canada

Keegan responded to my call for participants which they saw posted in a group they follow on social media. We agreed to meet at a coffee shop in Toronto. As I waited for Keegan to arrive, a patron at the coffee shop was experiencing medical distress. I rushed to help and call 911. While I was on the phone with the 911 operator, Keegan arrived and came to help. I recognized the shirt they said they would be wearing and asked if they were Keegan while we were helping the person in distress. Paramedics arrived, and we both agreed we needed a minute to sit and process what had happened before starting the interview. I ensured that they still wanted to continue with the interview, and they were clear that they did. I made a quick assessment to ensure that I was able to carry on as well.

Keegan works on issues of consent and sexual assault. They have participated in several protests in Toronto and raise awareness around trauma experienced by women and also queer and trans folks, and how this intersects with violence. They tell me that they've been doing this work since they left an abusive relationship five to seven years ago. They say that getting back into activist spaces has helped them reclaim themself.

When asked about the rewards of doing this work, Keegan says:

> It feels really interpersonal. It's about building a community of people who I don't feel alien to. A lot of the world doesn't fit with how I would like it to be and that can be really alienating, and so activist spaces are like one of those spots where there's shared values, shared goals, and a drive to do something about it.

They explain that a lot of the trauma they experienced was around people not acting. So activist spaces, where people are doing things, become a healing space.

In terms of challenges, Keegan says that incremental change – for example, when the work is not yet intersectional or anti-oppressive – is hard to deal with. Accountability, in terms of reflecting upon what they could do differently, is hard but necessary, they tell me. In doing their advocacy work, Keegan also thinks about who is erased, who is marginalized, who is not valued, and who is in danger.

Keegan's children are what give them hope. Their children have shown understanding about what it means to give consent, even when they are playing. Some days are hard because their children still live in a world that is oppressive. In talking about disability, they explain that they look at disability more holistically, and challenge notions of ability as the default.

> My lens is that gender-based violence often results in trauma, and trauma can be framed as a disability. It's tricky because my lenses are such that I feel like disability can be in the systems that we exist in, [and this] can be really Othering. The framing of disability naturally frames ability as the default and somehow better, and that doesn't work for me.

When asked about changes over time, Keegan says:

> I think some of the changes are environmental. There is a sense of threat, a sense of escalation, a sense that the work is essential in a way that really, it's ramped up since the 2016 election in the States. The rise of populism and the feeling of threat in my community particularly, the queer community, has skyrocketed. There are feelings of a lack of safety, and I think that there's a certain immediacy, a certain increase in frequency of protest and movements that I didn't see in the beginning.

Keegan ended by telling me:

> I think that I want to make sure that it's clear that this work for me is really personal, and that it comes from a place of trying to right things that are not rightable. There's no way of undoing stuff that happened. There's no way of erasing trauma. But the meaning-making that exists is powerful and world-changing and so activism for me is that meaning-making. It's building community in response to isolation. It's empowering which counteracts feeling powerless. It's the medicine and, yeah, I need it.

### Addressing intersectionality

Keegan's story shows the way that identity cannot be easily categorized or addressed as separate parts. Fran talks about this when she describes ways in which the disability movement did not want to address women's experiences because there was a fear it would split the movement. In fact, they did not want to address any additional layers of identity: gender, race, or sexuality. As previously noted by Molly, there is a lack of representation in the disability movement, which is still largely dominated by older, white, physically disabled men. Her observation that the voices of younger or gender non-conforming people are excluded speaks to inadequately addressing or understanding intersectionality. Fran has this to say about what gets addressed in education programmes even now:

> [In] a lot of disability studies programmes there isn't a gendered lens. You know, where you're going to see this is in women's studies, where they might have a women with disabilities course that is part of the curriculum in a broader gender studies programme, but I don't see the same focus in disability studies. I wonder why. I wonder why we aren't talking about sexuality. Yes, I know that we need to be looking at this work through an anti-oppressive lens, but I think that we need to really carve out space for marginalized folks within our own community to have access to this material and resources and scholarship.

According to some participants, there has been a failure to account for the ways in which our identities do not neatly fit into systems. For example, qualifying for support programmes is made more complicated by strict criteria that do not take an intersectional approach. Patricia, who previously worked with women with mental health disabilities in Toronto, says that sometimes people may have mental health disabilities along with chronic pain or physical disabilities. Charlie, who does similar work, explains the issue with the system:

> I feel like it's sometimes impossible to extricate any two aspects of someone's identity, like for folks who identify as having a disability and then are also experiencing issues related to their gender identity or sexuality. Of course, those things are happening in tandem and are like two parts of a whole person, and I think it's impossible to isolate based on one particular aspect of their marginalization. That's something that's in the neo-liberal system that we're working in that often tries, or organizations often try, to do that: they try to filter people out based on eligibility criteria that don't always acknowledge the messy complexities of identity.

Intersectionality is important because it provides a deeper understanding of oppression which is embedded in the very systems that support women and trans people with disabilities who experience violence. Sarah, in the United States, describes the intersectional approach that is embedded in her work, telling us that if you start from a place of inclusion it becomes embedded in the process, but she is also open about the challenges:

> I really try to be intersectional with my work as well. I also work and do some queer justice stuff and trying to bring all of that work together. I think that's it hard to do it on a large scale. I think that when it comes

to intersectionality it's kind of like a bottom-up sometimes. At my school, I'm the president of the Disability Identity Club and we have a specific person who's in charge of intersectionality and we always are trying to do events with the Black Student Union, with Union Latina and with the Queer Alliance.

I think creating those relationships on the ground I find really important because I think there are a lot of people who know how to use intersectional as the buzz word, but don't know how to put it to use …

Sarah talks about the importance of connecting with people with different identities and says,

Also just to refer to your question of how do I see myself fitting into that, I really try connect to some of these people who are higher up in the leadership and have been working longer, to try and look at them as a model to learn how do I apply a radical disability justice framework into what I'm already doing.

From this perspective, the historical and continued lack of representation of women and trans people with disabilities in anti-violence, gender, and disability movements addressed in the previous theme feeds into a lack of recognition about intersectionality as a way of working. If movements have trouble incorporating disability or gender, then it is challenging to start from a place of cooperation so that people representing all types of identity are included. In many ways, these themes overlap, influence, and perpetuate each other.

## Structural violence

Structural violence was one of the strongest themes to emerge from the interviews. I chose Patricia's story to introduce this theme because, not only does it feature prominently in her interview, but also Patricia raises several relevant and unique issues that contribute to the structural violence that women with disabilities, and those advocating with them, face.

### Patricia – Toronto, Canada

I met Patricia in grad school. She has been working in the area of women's mental health in Toronto since 2010. She also facilitates expressive arts groups with different organizations. As an art therapist, she works with women with mental health disabilities. She sees her work as creating space for people to give voice to their experiences using the arts. Before returning to school, Patricia worked in a supportive housing programme advocating for housing security and income support, while also supporting the women she worked with during landlord disputes or court procedures, writing support letters, advocating with women by liaising with their parole officers, and generally ensuring that the women could meet their basic needs.

When I asked Patricia what brought her to the work, she tells me she is a psychiatric survivor:

> I survived not only emotional distress of my own, but I also survived the services that were supposed to help me. That's also something that I need to recover from.

Going through this experience, Patricia thought there must be better ways to work with people and offer support. She came across professionals who were good people with good intentions who helped her. She remembers one art therapist who worked with her and, though she did not say much, she would take things in and accept them and use art as a different way of working. Patricia was fascinated by the art therapist and decided she wanted to do something similar, so she first pursued an undergraduate degree at OCAD[1], followed by a graduate diploma at the Toronto Art Therapy Institute. She did a placement at a public school and realized that some of her students and their parents were homeless. When she talked to her supervisor about how to help, her supervisor told her, 'that's not your problem, that's a social worker's problem.' Feeling very strongly about these issues, Patricia decided to do her master's in Social Work.

When I ask what keeps her hopeful, Patricia says it is people coming together, supporting each other, and realizing they have the answer within themselves; being able to move forward with people towards their preferred future. This comes out in the community when people create together, especially when people do not feel pressure for their creative work to turn out a particular way.

Patricia raises structural issues that are inherent in the systems that claim to support and protect women with mental health disabilities in times of crisis; she identifies working within a rigid system that works against people. She tells me that the way the system is set up intends to screen people out and disqualify them. People often have to identify with a pathologized image of being disabled in order to say they have a right to something. Interestingly, as a support worker, Patricia expresses discomfort with her role in that very system. She tells me:

> The system works against people all the time and it's not flexible. It's very rigid and a lot of times it feels like, even though on paper it says it's supportive, and it's supportive housing, right? But, a lot of times, it intends to screen out, it intends to disqualify, for people to not be able to get the benefit, for people to jump through hoops … align themselves with a really pathologized image of being disabled in order to say they have rights to something. So, that's very, actually, disheartening, and a lot of times it's also, knowing that I'm complicit, right? Because I am paid to do this, or I was paid to do this. And so, I benefit from the system that constructs people as inadequate.

She goes on to tell me that it was exhausting cooperating with the system she described. Patricia also talks about the challenge of funding given the way the system is set up to support people with disabilities. In talking about the Ontario Disability Support Program (ODSP), she says:

> In terms of the way that the systems determine qualification for benefits that would really support women to live a life that they want to live, and be more comfortable basically, and have basic needs met, have food on the table while being able to pay rent and afford, you know, a roof over their heads, and a door they can lock and feel safe. These things are not met, and people still have to almost beg, and that just repeats. A lot times the system ... just repeats the vicious cycle, but it repeats sort of the same dynamic of abuse too.

The system is traumatizing for the women Patricia worked with. She explains: 'When people go to, like, say, emerge[ncy] for a mental health crisis, people are still restrained, physically and chemically. Treated without consent, right? This is traumatizing.' Interestingly, Patricia tells me about decisions being made by people in positions of power impacting women with disabilities experiencing violence in ways that might not be immediately obvious:

> We're cutting library services and we think, 'Well, what does that have to do with violence against women?' A lot of women hang out at libraries because it's a safe place, it's cool in the summer, and it's warm in the winter. They go and read and it's good. It's something that they really value. I work with a lot of women who would just hang out at the library all day. It's safe. And so they're cutting it, right? They're cutting the hours. So, if the local library is not available, not open, how are they going to get to another library? ... we just got rid of tokens [to use the transit system], so they can't even get tokens from agencies, so I don't know what agencies are doing.

In addition to doing her PhD, Patricia currently works primarily in arts-based therapy. She has noticed over time more focus on mindfulness practices, body-based practices, 'not just in the mind, and it's not about retelling your story over and over again, and it's not about requiring women to tell their story of trauma.' Rather than focus solely on overcoming symptoms and the self as the problem, there still needs to be more focus on society. She explains, 'it's the misogyny and the patriarchy and the hetero-patriarchy that's the problem. There's not a lot of addressing of that.'

Patricia expresses concern that things are getting worse because shelters are closing and there are fewer spaces. There is less funding for food banks, emergency services, and other programmes. But there are also positive changes in terms of recognizing the arts and mindfulness practices as ways to support people to manage their lives and challenges, and intentionally focusing on trauma-informed practice, something which Patricia is centering as part of her current PhD work.

## *Forms and impacts of structural violence*

Patricia's story highlights the fact that structural violence can mean that the way systems are set up are inherently violent and that there are complications that arise from working within those systems. These systems may be social services (or support systems), education, employment, medical settings, and justice systems that do not meet the needs of women with disabilities. Structural violence can take place in movements as well. For example, if a person feels their experience is erased because it is not the default experience represented, that can be violent. We saw this with Keegan who talks about ability being framed as the default and that not working for them. Keegan says:

> How pathologizing and disability go together, these are the pieces where I don't identify with work specifically in disability. However, if I look at it in a more holistic way, of making sure that my experience is seen and not erased, if ability is going to be framed as the default anyway, then I'm sure as hell going to jump up and be, like, 'Actually, no, there are other experiences that exist, I challenge your space as default.'

Patricia gives us much to think about in terms of how support systems are set up to disadvantage people they claim to help. The organization of priorities and policies is an expression of structural violence. Charlie describes the support system in Toronto in much the same way as Patricia. Charlie says they are 'working with folks who are often very oppressed by the particular systems that we're trying to navigate through', and because of that they find themself working against this system at a very basic level by 'being a spokesperson and collaborating with [the women with mental health disabilities they work with] on their behalf in order to have their needs met and to empower them to have more choices in what their care looks like.' Charlie tells me about several instances in hospitals where they have had to advocate for women with mental health issues such as a patient being discharged without access to the appropriate supports at home, or a person going to hospital and finding her actual medical issue is overshadowed by her substance use. They tell me of a time when a client fell in the hospital and hit her head:

> I rushed to her side. Luckily, I happened to be there and three or four nurses at the nurses' stations were watching me and taking their time. They didn't make any sort of move to stand up and help her. It wasn't until I said, 'This person just fell and hit their head.' Which, normally, in hospitals they're all over that. They're super scared of falls and getting sued ... The way they talked to her, the way they looked at her, the way she was treated ... They weren't really seeing her as a patient that needed care. They were seeing her as somebody who was using drugs who clearly wasn't deserving the same kind of attention and urgency as another patient.

In other cases, perhaps, the people working within the support systems want to be helpful but they lack the resources to meet the needs of women with disabilities. See what Fran says about the shelter system in Toronto, for example (p. 54):

Molly in Winnipeg suggests that history follows us into the present and reinforces violence. She lives and works in a Canadian province where institutionalization, eugenics, and sterilization affecting people with disabilities has a significant and relatively recent history. She describes how this affects her today:

> I live in Manitoba and we're home to the last two institutions in Canada and that's hard, to exist under a system that still has those and that are so nearby ... The continuous haunting of all these institutions and our province that have these horrible histories and are home to eugenics and sterilization and continue to. But we're not involved in those conversations.

She explains the provincial government had recently given two of the large institutions twenty million dollars for renovations. She says that there is a need to keep people aware of the histories of these institutions. The work is also in honouring and acknowledging history:

> The Manitoba Developmental Centre used to be the Manitoba Home for Defectives and the School of Incurables and all these things. And so it's just keeping vigilant about keeping those voices in our conversation, and also never forgetting that they're there because that's part of it. Nobody in Winnipeg knows about residential institutions.

Karen, who is in Australia, referred to violence perpetrated by caregivers towards people with disabilities and also towards her when she spoke up about abuse. Karen responded to my call for participants because she wanted to speak about her experience as a female service provider with an invisible disability working in a system that is structurally violent. Karen worked at an institution primarily for autistic men, but also some women. When she began her position as a manager, she was given a tour of the facilities. Upon discovering a locked box being used as a form of punishment for the clients, she immediately became alarmed. When she tried to address this, the institution made it clear that if she continued with her line of questioning she would be left in situations with the male clients that might not be safe. It was Karen's opinion that a lack of training for caregivers was the root cause of violence perpetrated by care workers in Australia:

> In disability in Australia, you don't even need any qualifications to be working in this space. So, you kind of encourage this unprofessional environment that's potentially very informal anyway because the clients prefer it. There's a risk in that space of these boundaries constantly being crossed and not negotiated very well in some instances.

This type of violence impacts women with disabilities as well. Of note was the underlying assumption of the staff that the male clients could potentially be dangerous or could act in an unsafe manner towards Karen. Why this was the case is beyond the scope of my study, so I did not follow that line of questioning. Rather, I chose to focus on any cases of violence towards women with disabilities she may have encountered. Karen gives me one example that speaks strongly to how this system affects women with disabilities. It is the case of a 16-year-old girl with a disability:

> I had a family approach me and talk to me about sterilizing their teenage daughter and I asked them why they wanted to do that. They said because they were so worried that their daughter was going to come home from the respite centre pregnant … They thought that was a better option: to sterilize their daughter rather than deal with the abuse that was happening at the centre. I think that's what's happening in these environments, that people are so desperate for help and support that they put up with so much abuse and violence … The parents actually thought they were protecting their child rather than doing anything harmful. Because they just couldn't deal with the addition of having to report what they were really worried about in terms of the abuse and neglect that their daughter was experiencing. Just so that they could get some respite.

The parent's consideration of sterilization is symbolic of the large-scale failure of a system that positions institutional environments as respite for families. Instead, these institutions are unnatural environments and cause harm. Karen says that providers are failing their clients:

> You know, the abuse is so well known and institutionalized and part of the disability culture that people are going to such extremes to address it. I think when we don't have an organic or natural environment that we're in, and we exclude people with disabilities from community and mainstream, and we create these unnatural environments for people. This is the outcome of that.

When you have these constructed spaces, the system fails to fully support people with disabilities and their families, and abuse occurs. Like Karen, Molly raises structural problems related to service providers in Canada. In talking about disclosing sexual abuse, Molly says she does not think women with disabilities have been given space to disclose because the abuse complaints

> … would be against care workers, and drivers, and all those people that we still have to interact with every single day. So, we don't have that space because we've been saying this for so long, and nobody's been listening, and, legally, nobody cares. In Manitoba, we have a current human rights violation against our Handi-trans drivers because

they're constantly accused of sexual violence and then still have the right to drive you the next day. So, you can accuse a driver of harassment or violence or whatever, and then he will be notified and will still be able to pick you up the next day.

The implications of this are quite serious. Women with disabilities often rely upon accessible transportation services to get to their jobs, medical appointments, social gatherings, and other places. For them, it is an essential service. The person providing the service becomes a threat first by sexually harassing a user, and then again by having continued isolated interactions with that user after she has made a formal complaint against him. This puts women in an impossible position.

Sarah, a student advocate in the United States, raised the important point that many forms of therapy and restraints are acts of violence towards people with disabilities Molly, in Manitoba, also raises violence towards women with psychiatric diagnoses characterized as concern for safety:

> Ongoing locking up of women who demonstrate any questioning … But nobody is having those conversations about austerity governments. They're not like, 'This is violent, we're increasing policing of people who don't need that.' … How do we even engage people in those conversations when society has been neglecting it for so long?

A trend among the participants who discussed psychiatric diagnoses or mental health issues is a framing of people with such diagnoses as dangerous. Any violence perpetrated by caregivers or those working in institutions is framed as treatment and, therefore, deemed acceptable.

Other participants also talk about how attitudes towards people with disabilities often interact with structures to create additional barriers and challenges. This could be at societal level. Amal, in Yemen, describes women with disabilities being isolated at home and kept away from society. This could also play out within other structures in society. Take, for example, the education system, Usha in India tells me about her work to get more blind and visually impaired children into schools. She explains that when she asked one girl's parents to allow her to go to school they say no because they don't believe in school and that it is far from their home (See Usha's story on page 119).

I would argue that preventing a child from going to school is in itself violent. But the education system can itself also be structurally violent. Jane, in Kenya, describes struggling in school because it was not accessible (See Jane's Story on page 132).

Misti, in Bangladesh, describes some of the educational barriers she faced,

> The university denied me to be admitted in their university due to my disability. They say that the academic building is not accessible so they could not allow me study there. So, I drop out and I go back to my hometown again.

One participant describes her experience in the workplace:

> I also try to track the opportunity to get a job, but it was very difficult to get the job and sometimes, many times, I get the job and when I went to the office and the boss, he also tried sexual exploitation. They always try to. Many [types of] discrimination. I always object to that thing. It is not easy situation. It's a very difficult situation for women with disabilities.

In other cases, the way that police treat survivors of abuse is an additional violence enacted upon the survivor and this is something that advocates and community organizers encounter in their work. Elizabeth, in Ghana, tells the story of a young blind girl who was asked to go back and identify her attacker after she reported her assault (I will return to the details when discussing access to justice shortly). Tika, in Nepal, describes a similar situation arising from lack of understanding about accessibility within systems:

> There is no sign language interpreter, there is no assistant, there is no accessible facility for the victims of violence. And sometimes a blind woman, if she is raped and she cannot identify the perpetrator, and the lawyer, the police, the government, and those who are working in legal mechanisms, they don't know about that thing. They really ignore that issue. You know? They try to treat women with disabilities equally to other women. They think, 'Why do they need different technique, treatment?' That is the thing.

Structural violence is complex, comprehensive, and evasive. The participants I interviewed describe violence in accessing and qualifying for services, violence in the way their experiences of abuse are handled, barriers to accessing education – which is a fundamental right, and violence perpetrated by people working within the various systems women and trans people with disabilities interact with.

## Rights

### Karen – Australia

Karen Burgess works in the disability sector in Australia. She runs four Facebook groups with a total membership of 20,000 people for the purpose of informing others about the National Disability Insurance scheme that was developed in 2013. She volunteers, doing advocacy work, alongside a career in front-line and management work. She has two professional roles: one is to train people how to work with people with disabilities. She also designs, implements, and manages a range of programmes which support inclusion for people with disabilities. She has been working on disability issues since 1993 when, as an early childhood educator, she worked specifically with children with disabilities.

When I ask Karen how she got her start, she says that she has a brother with a mental health disability and she herself has dyslexia and dysgraphia, so she has very personal experience with disability. Karen's current main area of focus is working with men who have what she calls 'behaviours of concern or behaviours that are associated with a disability'. She approached my research questions from the perspective of a woman working in complex environments. She worked with primarily male colleagues who took the approach of using force or physical restraint, which she was opposed to.

> When you're opposing a type of strategy, working with men in a male-dominated environment, using physical restraints it could become even more complex for a woman and, certainly, the toxic dialogue that you've got with your colleagues in terms of the approaches that were being used professionally was, you know, sometimes not as supportive as you would hope and, in some cases, were threatening and hostile.

Karen tells me about being a front-line manager for an autism day programme that serviced primarily men, but also had some women attending. Within three days of working at the site, she asked about a box in the corner of the room which she was told was used for disciplinary purposes – by locking people in it. The classroom where the box was located would also be locked. She reported the box to her employer. But her concerns were not taken seriously, so she reported it to the Disability Commissioner and the police. As a result, she lost her job. She tells me that when she was reporting the incident, she was told by people she worked with that, if she continued with her line of questioning, they would happily leave her in unsafe environments with clients and that maybe an accident would happen. She says that part of the issue is that violence in the disabilities sector happens within a structure and environment that also needs to be addressed.

Karen raises additional concerns with violence towards women working in the disability sector. Reporting concerns in the sector could lead to violence being perpetrated towards them. As noted earlier, she believes there is violence in the disability sector in Australia because the environment of care is informal and what she describes as unprofessional. She has also worked with men with physical disabilities who have sexualized her or became violent towards her as a worker. When I asked Karen about the women attending the centre where she worked, she explains:

> I don't believe it was very safe for the women at all, and that informed part of my initial complaint to the people that were there. And I was very concerned with the women who were there. But that formed all parts of my complaint in my original raising of my concerns about what was happening at the centre.

I ask Karen what keeps her hopeful and she says that there is an understanding of disability in mainstream culture, and it's no longer just on the fringe. People are accepting and accommodating. Karen tells me that her disability is invisible but that she has been aware of it since she was very young. She says:

> I don't have anything visually that people can see. I just kind of feel like the disability exists only when other people see it and complain about it. I don't have an idea that my disability is a problem until other people tell me it's a problem. I guess it's because I actually have such a good self-ego and a good confidence about it that it doesn't bother me ... The perception of my disability only lives in the perception of others.

She references dealing with people in authority as a challenge. Decision-makers are not acting as quickly or as efficiently as they could. In addressing the violence against people with a disability, there is a lack of action which prevents people with disabilities who experience violence from getting support they need. Karen tells me about concerns with violence against women with disabilities in group homes: in one case, a sex criminal had been hired and was assaulting residents. Regarding the concerned family of the 16-year-old girl whose family thought sterilization[2] was the best solution to avoid her getting pregnant at the respite care centre, Karen points out:

> You know it's just horrible. And they were talking with me very matter-of-factly, so they must have rationalized it and already thought about and deduced that this was better. They weren't upset about this discussion at all. They were very rational and calm about it, and they clearly had thought very heavily about it.

Karen points out that this is a bigger issue:

> That really says the community is failing. These providers are absolutely failing their clients if clients feel like they have to do that ... I think we don't have an organic or natural environment and, often by design, people with disabilities are excluded from their community and mainstream society. There is a great need to create natural environments for people with disabilities and with the focus for removing a number of barriers.

Karen says she has seen more women with disabilities in leadership positions, and there is more support for women with disabilities so they are able to accept leadership positions. So, for example, in Australia a lot of women with disabilities are speaking out about women's issues and violence and sterilization. Also, at the time of the interview, she says the National Disability Insurance scheme seems to be more advantageous for men than women, so they have started to address that. She says, 'I've seen a lot more opportunities for women with disabilities to be able to represent other women with disabilities. So that's been a positive change.' She acknowledges that it is usually men with disabilities representing the voices of people with disabilities in the media. In terms of what keeps her hopeful, she talks about the Australian Royal Commission into Disability and Violence[3], which was just starting. At the time of the interview, she and others in the disability community were preparing stories to document violence against people with disabilities.

Karen ends by telling me that she had a hearing and used parliamentary privilege to make sure the story about the disciplinary box was told. She says, 'I think it's important to use my name, too, because it keeps people very on point to know that I'm continuing to raise this and continuing to talk about this and I haven't forgotten and I'm not going to let anyone forget what's happened.'

### Rights work

Karen talks about addressing rights in a number of areas, from the rights of people working in the system, to those of people interacting with these systems. A number of other participants identify women's awareness about their rights as a challenge. Elizabeth, in Ghana, emphasizes the importance of improving self-advocacy skills among women with disabilities so that they are able to advocate for rights as women and as people with disabilities. She refers to rights legislation:

> For example, the UNCRPD, the United Nations Convention [on the Rights of Persons with Disabilities], we also have a domestic violence act so we build their capacities, we make them aware of those legislations so that they can use those legislations, with their knowledge, to demand their rights any time their rights are trampled upon in the communities.

When I ask Amal about changes in the area of gender-based violence in the disability community over time, she notes women with disabilities have increased their societal participation and awareness of their rights. The existence of rights legislation does not necessarily guarantee that rights will be achieved. Fran expresses this concern as a challenge:

> What I say to my students, often times, is you know these are the rights that we have but don't think that these are guaranteed. Yes, they're on paper but we know many people don't enjoy these rights and they can slip away very easily as we are seeing in the US and what's happening there with the ADA [Americans with Disabilities Act] and Medicare. I think that we have to continue to be vigilant and I don't know how we get younger people to be part of that.

Knowing what our rights are, though, can be a basis for empowerment. On a personal level, Jane says she feels stronger because she knows when she has had her rights violated as a woman with a disability. That said, she also expresses concerns that rights instruments such as the Convention on the Elimination of all forms of Discrimination against Women, may not adequately address women with disabilities:

Misti makes a point related to this: at the time of the interview there was only one woman on the Committee for the Convention on the Rights of Persons with Disabilities, making representation an ongoing issue. Since then, there has been increased representation on the Committee.

Some participants named specific rights violations as challenges they face in their advocacy work. One participant makes the point that, often, women with disabilities are not in control of their bodies: 'The rights of people with disabilities to have sexual relationships, to have romantic relationships is absolutely tied to the right to not have sexual relationships, to not be controlled by partners.' Reproductive health was mentioned as a right that women with disabilities are often denied.

Molly says that even if human rights violations happen, the complaints are made within a violent system that does not guarantee the safety of the people filing the claims – as was the case with the Handi-trans driver who was still transporting the woman who filed sexual harassment complaints against him. This instance could also be filed under the next theme which is access to justice.

## Access to justice

### Elizabeth – Ghana

Elizabeth reached out to me after seeing my call for participants on social media. She works with the Ghana Blind Union as a programme manager for inclusion. Ghana Blind Union is a membership-based organization. Elizabeth coordinates the organization's advocacy activities which are geared toward inclusion of blind and partially sighted persons in mainstream services such as education, health, and employment. The organization also has a programme specifically for blind or partially sighted women.

Elizabeth has been doing disability advocacy work for 12 years. She was trained as a teacher and became interested in disability advocacy while she was doing adolescent reproductive health work. One day, during a radio call-in programme, she received a call from a young blind girl who had asked a stranger to help her navigate to the bus. The stranger lured her to his room and raped her. The girl called into the radio show because she had no one to turn to, and she asked to speak to Elizabeth off air.

Elizabeth tells me she became interested in her case and followed up on it. It was because of this that she began to think about disability in her own awareness programmes working with youth and girls. She was then contacted by another disability organization in Ghana to do a radio outreach programme to help sensitize the public to disability issues. This is where her work began. Now she works on programmes geared to capacity building and advocacy, and addressing the challenges blind women and women with visual impairments face. When a woman loses her sight, she is supported in learning new ways to manage family and mothering responsibilities. Sometimes mothers will have their children taken away, so the Ghana Blind Union raises awareness about human rights legislation.

When asked about challenges, Elizabeth speaks first about breaking through barriers and stigma attached to having a disability. She also describes an ongoing need to do advocacy in a challenging policy landscape that includes discrimination and exclusion by service providers.

She says the moments when women realize who they are and make efforts to transform their lives are rewarding, and seeing people being able to achieve a level of leadership. What keeps her hopeful is Ghana's commitments to local and national legislation, as well as the Sustainable Development Goals to narrow the gaps between people with and without disabilities. Though there are international developments, and national commitments to funding and support, she says her organization will continue to advocate for grassroots capacity building.

She also raises access to justice as a concern. Elizabeth ends with an explanation about the Access to Justice programme that works on the systemic barriers institutions of justice have in place that limit access for women with visual impairments.

> Working with women with disabilities at the grassroots, I realize that there's a lot more to be done because capacity, confidence, and bringing out the issues are key to their realization of their fundamental human rights. So, for me, that is what we are committed to do as an organization and then, like I said, we have a programme we call Access to Justice. You can imagine the kind of barriers that our own systems, institutions of justice, have put in place to limit access to women with visual impairment.

To demonstrate her point, Elizabeth tells me the story of a young woman in Ghana who sought justice after a sexual assault and describes the extent to which ableism is embedded not only in the system, but also in the attitudes of individuals working in the justice system:

> Let me take, for example, the police service in Ghana. We have a situation in one of our programmes where one woman reported that she was raped. She walked to the police station to report the case and then, if I could quote her, she said, "Madam can you please? I cannot see. And the police officer on duty asked me to go back to my community and then spy and ensure that my suspect is available before I come back to report to them, then they can go and effect the arrest. I cannot see. How can I identify even if the person is available or not?" So, this could clearly tell you that our systems of justice in place are not properly incorporating the needs of persons with disability ... So, there is lots of work to be done as far as justice and human rights issues are concerned.

Elizabeth continues to work on awareness raising and advocacy with blind women and women with low vision to get access to supports, services, and legal remedies.

### Access to justice

Elizabeth's story demonstrates one of a multitude of ways that accessing justice for survivors with disabilities can be challenging. Access to justice came up as a challenge time and again in the interviews. See, for example, Karen's desire to see convictions for people committing violence against men and women with disabilities, and her hopes that the Royal Commission will help bring about change, expressed in the next section.

After seeing many women with disabilities in the community experience violence and not subsequently have adequate access to legal recourse, some participants made this a priority in their work. A participant in Kenya tells me that one of the hardest things is knowing that women and girls with disabilities experience sexual abuse and the cases go unreported because there are many barriers to accessing justice. Molly, in Winnipeg, talks about increased reporting of violence against women in general, but questions whether or not women with disabilities are included in the figures reported by the Royal Canadian Mounted Police (RCMP):

> Looking at the rates of people reporting to the RCMP [people said], 'They went up by like 20% during the time of MeToo.' ... It doesn't feel like it's improving for us as disabled women. It feels like this growing divide almost and, yeah, it sucks to be included in conversations about it being better when it's like, 'Better for who?'

Molly describes reporting abuse and then being forcibly institutionalized as a result. One would expect to get access to justice but, instead, women with disabilities risk being institutionalized themselves. Misti explains the challenges in Bangladesh, saying that when women with disabilities are abused:

> So, we try to make collaboration with the law, legal-aid-providing agencies, and we have good networking with them. We have advocacy with the lawyers and the bar association who are practicing in the court. We also have some advocacy meeting with our judges. We try to create sensitivity among them. How to provide the legal support to the girls and women with disabilities ... How to provide the legal support to the disabled people in the court ... So, the girls and women with disabilities and families, they can understand how they will go to police station, go to court, go to lawyer, and how they get justice. This is instrumental, actually.

Tika spoke about the number of women with disabilities who have experienced violence and abuse in Nepal. Her organization works to support victims: keeping them safe and helping them get access to justice when they report their cases. However, they are not always successful. She tells me:

> It is always difficult to get the remedy. We have no court specific mechanisms. Court has to decide for the remedy, but victim she is always waiting for that opportunity. And never meet that point. That is always problem, [there are] many problems in Nepal.

We will hear Sarah's story in the next section, but it is important to mention here that Sarah left her first school because she was assaulted and there was no chance of her abuser facing any consequences. The justice systems women rely upon are inherently ableist. Community advocates and organizers do the work of addressing these systems to make them accessible.

## Policy and government commitment challenges

### Sarah – United States

Sarah is a 21-year-old university student in the United States who does sexual violence and disability advocacy work. Her sexual violence advocacy work takes place primarily at her school. Her disability advocacy extends more broadly. Sarah tells me that while at her first college, she experienced abuse herself and this is why she became involved in advocacy. The college had an issue of prevalent sexual violence on campus, and yet it was swept under the rug. She transferred universities because the environment at her former school was unsafe:

> That's the reason that I actually ended up leaving that school, because that culture was so bad and also, kind of, to get away from my abuser because I knew that that was not an environment that could keep me from him, and I had no shot at getting him expelled or anything.

She transferred to a university in another state and is now majoring in disability studies. She currently works in the anti-violence office at her university where a student staff of thirteen, and two full-time staff members, do counselling, advocacy, and prevention work. Sarah focuses on advocacy on campus, working to support survivors, and creating a more supportive atmosphere on campus.

In terms of her disability advocacy, she started when she was twelve but became disabled, she says, when she was sixteen. She started advocating for inclusion at her school and, as she got older, she got involved in what she calls the more radical aspects of disability. Sarah works broadly on deinstitutional-ization and issues of involuntary commitment, while also working with the independent living movement and disability pride movement in her state. She says she enjoys the pride movement because her disability is one of her favourite things about herself, and she is proud of who she is. Because of this, she focuses a lot on identity and empowerment issues. Sarah also does a lot of cross-disability organizing. She is one of only two participants to speak about having a physical and a psychiatric disability, and her desire to bring those aspects of disability together in the community.

When I asked Sarah how long she has been doing violence and disability work specifically she tells me about the impact that the Ferguson protests[4] had on her. She says:

> I would say that I started getting involved in it a little bit when I was about 16 after Ferguson happened. That was the police brutality and that; I always call it my political awakening because that is when I stopped being like, 'Oh, be nice to each other.' I was more radical. I started getting more political and so, kind of, in that discussion of police brutality I became really interested in looking at violence because it was something that we weren't talking about that much. But so many victims of police brutality have disabilities. And then, when I went to college and I started working on sexual violence on our campus, immediately I was like, 'We need to talk about disability more when we're talking about this' because I definitely felt like, in my experience, my disability played a part in my victimization.

Sarah was able to think about the political context around her and how it impacted people with disabilities. She says that even now, when she is doing anti-violence work on campus, she is the one who is raising the issue of how it impacts people with disabilities. As part of her work, she is on the violence and abuse sub-committee for the National Council of Independent Living and identifies this as an area where her two interests have come together.

When I ask Sarah about the challenges she faces in her work, she raises the important point that violence towards people with disabilities is sometimes committed in the name of therapy, citing things like ABA therapy and restraints in hospitals. Sarah tells me that, at the time of our interview, she had just met with a congressman to talk about legislation that she wanted him to oppose because she felt it was intended to increase the number of beds in psychiatric hospitals. The congressman's view was that parents needed more help caring for their family members who might be a threat to themselves or others. She argued that increasing institutionalization would just increase violence. During our interview, she makes the point that, when a person has a disability, violent treatments are characterized as therapeutic.

There is also a strategic importance of raising disability rights and violence issues as soon as new elections conclude. She explains her rationale for this strategy:

> I really like doing federal-level work and I think that I've gotten to a point where I have a lot of contacts at the federal level. Our State just flipped a bunch of seats in congress this past election and that's been a really good opportunity for me to, kind of, get in right from the beginning … a lot of the older congressmen are yes men and they'll be like, 'Yeah, yeah, yeah, I'll do that.' And then don't.

I ask Sarah what motivates her to do this difficult work. She tells me that there is a dual motivation for her. The first is that she can't not do something. She says:

> If you don't do anything then it feels like it's out of your control. But, when you're doing something, you're like, 'Well at least I can do this.' I'm doing my part and I think it makes you a little bit less angry because you're at least doing something.

Sarah's second motivation is that she feels a sense of healing through helping. The work is especially emotionally taxing because she has post-traumatic stress disorder (PTSD) as a result of the kinds of violence she is advocating against. She says that, for her, it's more about advocating for other people but, when she is fighting for other survivors, she is also fighting for herself.

Sarah then tells me about the impact of being part of a movement. She says the people she works with are supportive and passionate about the same issues. When they start to feel emotionally drained, they talk to each other about ways of coping and draw strength from knowing there are other people out there supporting the work and what they are doing. She explains:

> There are just all these people who are so passionate about [this work], and we were talking about this after the Kavanaugh hearings.[5] Things were really hard for a lot of us because we were so emotionally drained, and we started to talk about how do you keep yourself motivated and hopeful, and not just fall into despair.

She says that doing this work helps give her a sense of control and like she is doing her part.

Sarah tells me that the changes she has seen over time have only been slight. A report done by Joe Shapiro with National Public Radio (NPR) two years earlier highlighted seven times higher rates of sexual assault among women and men with intellectual disabilities. Sarah says the accessible format of NPR makes these issues more available to the public. She points out:

> I definitely do feel like people are at least mentioning disability because at first it was like, 'No, women are more likely to experience this'. Then it was women and people of colour, and now we're starting to see disability included in that which I think is really great.

Sarah returns to the issue of forced therapies. She says that, while more people are advocating against these therapies, the result is that people who are in favour of them fight back even harder. She has a positive framing for this:

> I always look at that as a good thing because, if we look histori- cally, when there's that major push back it means that we're doing

something or we're making progress. When I see people getting really angry and defending this stuff very passionately, that means that we're actually making progress because if we weren't a threat to them, they wouldn't care.

Disability justice is something that Sarah feels passionate about. She says this has been an important part of the disability movement as it seeks to involve intersecting groups which have been previously silenced in the disability community. She also thinks disabled women and non-binary disabled people are talking a lot more about violence and hate crimes in the disability community. She feels leaders used to focus on issues that were politically strategic and easier to address, and now she sees leaders talking about issues that are problematic.

Sarah speaks specifically about the importance of taking an intersectional approach to her work. She does queer justice work and is also president of the Disability Identity Club at her Students' Union. They try to do events with other groups on campus like the Black Student Union, Union Latina, and the Queer Alliance. She feels that building these relationships is important because intersectionality is more than a buzz word, it is something to be put into practice. She says:

> If you're working intimately and closely with people of all different identities, intersectionality just becomes kind of seamless. If you have leaders, five leaders who are all white cis gender men, then you're going to have to work to bring in those other frameworks. But if you have a queer woman, a non-binary person, a man of colour, you have all these different identities in there already, then it's just going to naturally come together. So that's really how I've tried to do things.

Sarah works on gender-based violence in the disability community from several vantage points. She works on campus as an advocate, she works in the community against abusive practices and therapies, and she advocates at the government level against negative attitudes and treatment of people with disabilities, and on anti-violence work with a view towards ensuring that other people do not have to experience some of the things she has.

### Policy and government commitment challenges

I chose to tell Sarah's story to introduce this theme because of her commitment to meeting with government officials and working at the federal level to advocate for change. All but two participants raised concerns about policy or government commitment to addressing gender-based violence in the disability community. This was noted across contexts and countries. Elizabeth, in Ghana, describes:

> Lukewarm attitudes on the part of policy makers and even from family members, discrimination and exclusion on the part of service providers,

and I say some consciously and some unconsciously ... The major challenge on the part of our work is governments not seeing disability as a priority and therefore making the appropriate strategies and then budget allocations for disability programmes ...

She goes on to say that, even when there are policies at the international level, they do not trickle down to communities:

We have the policies, but we have to commit the funding to build capacities at the regional, the national, and the local level. Those ones are not, let me say, forthcoming, or properly targeted. We have some break somewhere ... But when we come to the national level, we have made the national government and then other stakeholders support building capacity at the community levels. Also, support and commitment are not forthcoming. So that is where we have the break because when we are developing the top and then [those lower] down are still deficient, you see that those who really need the capacity are not getting it.

A lack of government prioritization can mean funding challenges for disability organizations who are already operating with a limited capacity. Fran talks about this during her interview. Even when there are people within the government who seem committed to making funding available, retro-fitting shelters can be expensive. It's not just that there isn't commitment to making it a priority, but there are also more funding cuts. Misti, in Bangladesh, describes progress with including disability in government priorities and explains that 'some policy intervention is now positive for the disability issues but there are so many gaps at the implementing level so we're trying to talk with government and the implementing agency to work it rightly.' Similarly, Molly describes policy challenges related to funding in Winnipeg, particularly around mental health and institutionalization. She notes a misdirection of funds:

I think like we've recently invested so much money in mental health care in Canada. Manitoba got like 40 million dollars, but they still cut all the services and psychiatric institutions and didn't use it for rehabs and instead used it to increase security in psych wards, in psych institutions.

So, even when funding is given, sometimes it is not directed to the most effective priorities. Tika, in Nepal, describes extensive work that she and her organization do to train government departments and officials on disability inclusion but, she says:

We are still advocating and lobbying to the government for making separate laws, separate mechanisms to address violence against women with disabilities ... Still the government has no specific policy, and if they have a policy, no implementation. That is a problem.

Though Jane talked about increased participation in elections, she also raises concerns about the barriers that still exist:

> At the political level we have seen women being nominated as members of parliament, members of senate, members of county assemblies, but that is only at nomination level. When it comes to election, nobody wants to have women with disabilities. Not even wanting, I don't have capacity to go do the vigorous campaign that one has to do. I don't have even an office. So, there are still gaps that need to be bridged.

Keegan, in Toronto, says that when the elections in the US happened, there was a sense of escalation, a need to do more advocacy with the rise of populism. They say, 'the feeling of threat in my community, particularly the queer community, has skyrocketed. The feelings of lack of safety, and I think that there's a certain immediacy, an increase in frequency of protest and movements.'

On a more individual or personal level, the way that policy decisions affect services has an impact on women with disabilities who are experiencing violence. Patricia is a trained social worker in Toronto and has worked in supportive housing. She has seen the policy environment hinder the everyday lives of the women she has worked with. She gives practical examples of the ways in which various services impact women, sometimes in ways that are not immediately obvious. She explains:

> There may be changes in the really specialized services that either require really long wait times or a lot of money. But the most marginalized women, the services they use – like ODSP, foodbank, hospital emergency services – there's no change at all. If anything, it's getting worse because of the funding cuts that we're experiencing continually and they're worsening in Ontario because of the premier we have ...

Karen in Australia speaks about using upcoming government commitments to address a previous lack of accountability for abuse towards women in the disability community:

> We've got a Royal Commission into Disability and Violence coming up in Australia. We're preparing our stories and we're getting ready to document and really shine a light on this type of violence that's been happening ... and I really want to see some criminal convictions come about. Like, I really want to see people who have been abusing people and women with a disability to be held to account for their behaviour and what has happened. I think the Royal Commission will shine a torch on that and really bring about the changes that we need within the industry.

Finally, Usha, whose story will be told in the next section, tells me a story which highlights a problematic way that government policies can mix with negative attitudes to affect women with disabilities. She tells me about a young girl whose life was at risk. The government had a policy that if people lost loved ones during a cyclone in one region, the family could be compensated. The young girl overheard her family plotting to throw her into the river and claim that she died during the cyclone in order to get compensation. This is an alarming and important kind of situation that disability advocates face in dealing with gender-based violence.

According to the participants I interviewed, policy and government priorities that do not consider the specific needs of women with disabilities in violent situations have negative impacts for the women, but also for the people working to affect change. As we have seen, the challenges that arise which affect women with disabilities experiencing violence in predictable, and in some not-so-predictable, ways creates additional challenges for the advocates.

Identifying the various experiences these participants have faced in their work was, in some ways, the more straightforward part of analysing these interviews. The more challenging task has been to present these themes separately because they overlap, impact, and influence each other. Take, for example, the negative attitudes discussed at the beginning of this chapter. These negative attitudes permeate society and contribute to the structural violence the participants discussed. In much the same way, negative attitudes can combine with government policies to have negative impacts on women and trans people with disabilities.

Another example of overlap is the lack of representation in movements and inadequate addressing of intersectionality. This may stem from the false belief that addressing more than one aspect of identity and associated oppression could take away from existing efforts to address gender issues or disability issues. Similarly, rights, access to justice, and a lack of government commitment could be addressed collectively because they influence each other.

Some of these experiences could be framed as contributing to transformations as well. Participant experiences may be a motivation to move forward, or they may provide an avenue to create change. For example, using a rights-based approach to gender-based violence in the disability community is one way that movements can use rights, justice, and government policies to address common concerns. The participants primarily speak about these issues as challenges and so I have chosen to focus on their representation in order to honour their work and stories. I will turn now to the transformative aspects of the work and situate them within social movement organizing around gender-based violence in the disability community.

## Notes

1.  OCAD University formerly known as The Ontario College of Art and Design in 2002–2010
2.  There is a degree of protection and regulation regarding sterilization of children and adults with disabilities, but there is currently no

law in Australia that prohibits sterilization. See https://dpoa.org.au/factsheet-sterilisation/

3.  Royal Commission into Violence, Abuse, Neglect and Exploitation of People with Disability was established in April 2019 to investigate violence, abuse, neglect, and exploitation of people with disabilities. The final report with recommendations to improve relevant laws, policies, structures and practices to the Australian government is planned for April 2022. See https://disability.royalcommission.gov.au/

4.  In 2014, a police officer fatally shot Michael Brown in Ferguson, Missouri. This sparked debates in the United States about police violence towards African Americans and use of force. The officer involved in the shooting was not indicted on any charges. The Ferguson protests garnered international attention. See, for example, the BBC's coverage here: https://www.bbc.com/news/world-us-canada-30193354

5.  In 2018, Brett Kavanaugh was nominated for the US Supreme Court. Three women, including Christine Blasey Ford, came forward with allegations of sexual assault by Kavanaugh. Four days of public hearings were held in September 2018 to investigate the allegations. Kavanaugh was appointed to the US Supreme Court in October 2018. Several media outlets covered the hearings at the time. See for example, The Washington Post  https://www.washingtonpost.com/politics/2018/09/27/takeaways-kavanaugh-hearing-so-far/

# CHAPTER 5
# Transformations

Education surfaces in different ways as a supportive part of advocacy work on gender-based violence in the disability community. Some participants emphasize the importance of getting an education; others focus on the importance of supporting others to get an education; and still others do anti-violence and disability work in university settings. When I ask participants what keeps them motivated and hopeful, they identify seeing their experiences reflected in the work, wanting a better situation for others, seeing a raised awareness about gender-based violence against people with disabilities, having support from the community, and improved advocacy. The next section will discuss these themes in detail.

Transformative aspects of doing gender-based violence work in the disability community can be viewed in terms of the factors that have supported community organizers to advocate for their rights. There are personal transformations as a result of doing the work. And then there are the positive outcomes for the movement and for people with disabilities affected by gender-based violence.

In terms of factors that support participants to advocate for their rights and motivate them to do the work, access to education, wanting a better situation for others, and community support all feature prominently, as does an outcome for the movement – raised awareness of the importance of including women and trans people with disabilities. I will start with education.

## Education

### Usha – Hyderabad, India

I met Usha in Hyderabad, India, in 2018. She was the first person I interviewed for my Ph.D dissertation project. I interviewed her while travelling between meetings in the city, and our conversation flowed very naturally. I was able to learn a great deal about Usha and her work. Usha was born to a royal family in India where the girls were traditionally home-schooled but, because they lived in a city, her sisters went to school. As a blind child, Usha was unable to attend because the school was inaccessible. Her father's friends suggested a school away from their home city where Usha could study. When she was six years old her father supported her to attend. Usha excelled at school, but her traditional grandparents did not like her to be in school as she was approaching her teenage years. In fact, they did not like her to be outside of the home at all. So Usha was then home-schooled in the traditional way. She was a curious girl and would ask her younger sisters to read books to her when they were studying, then she would ask them questions to see what they remembered.

Usha and her family moved to an area that was heavily influenced by General Motors and an American refinery company. Many people who lived there were from the United States, Usha tells me. When she was 19, people began to point out that she was bright and would ask her father why she was not studying. They told her about an entrance exam for a degree programme. Usha's friends helped her prepare for the exam by reading the material to her. She was accepted into the programme and graduated in three years. She then went on to do a master's in literature and one in education. Here she learned how to teach blind children and was then given a job at a school. Because Usha was from a royal family, her savings and earnings were her own. From a young age she would buy things for the servant's children then, as a teacher, she would help pay for books or school fees, going so far as to buy a house for some of the young girls to stay in while she was supporting them to get an education.

It is Usha's work at the school that catches my attention. She worked with children who were blind or had little sight. She supported 15 girls in going through school. She chose from very poor or needy families. She tells me:

> I love to play with the children and correct them, train them properly in making crafts because we had a lot of total loss of vision children when I joined. But, now these days, you know, because of the improvement of medication, most of the children have a little sight. They can see. They are not totally blind. But I had a lot of totally blind children and I wanted them all to be like me – independent. Don't depend on anybody for anything, so that's the reason I taught them.

Usha tells me that her father's support was instrumental in her getting an education. What is interesting is that Usha recognized her independence and then wanted the same for other children like her. Her altruism in wanting to help others is notable. Her work was not easy. She tells me that her school administrator would send her out into the rural areas to find young girls to be educated. She tells me one story that needs to be told here:

> I went to one village, a totally tribal area called Araku Valley near Vishaka district. So, there we heard that there was one blind child. I went to see there. You know, the child was tied with a rope to one pole and there was some food and water just like how you would put for a dog or something. She was just going about here and there, that child, visually impaired child. I really started crying looking at that child. How could the people do this? Like an animal just tied the rope to the pole and left. So, I went to the *panchayat*'s house and I asked him, 'What do her parents do?' They said, 'They are field workers. They just go to earn their

livelihood. This child may fall into any of those pits.' They have ground wells in the fields ... So, they think that she may slip into that. So, every day they do that and go to work and in the evening they come back. Instead of only having visual impairment, that girl she couldn't talk or move about freely like others because the whole day she was just tied up like that.

It's just too much. And I explained to them that we have a good school where she can study, she can learn. They said, 'No, no, no we don't believe in all that schools and all. It's very far. We can't put her in any school because she can't see. What will she study? What will she do?' I said, 'No it's nothing. You just come with me. You bring your child and one of you come with us to the school. You'll see there. Then put her in the school.' That girl, I brought that day with the parents and with great difficulty we put her in school. She turned out to be a very good student and she would sing beautifully. She had a sweet voice, you know. So, we taught her. We corrected all her mannerisms ... She was six years old, that child.

As an example of community organizing, this story encapsulates the various ways that women with disabilities organize to end violence. In this instance, Usha worked with her school, even went to the community leaders, and cooperated with the family to get this young girl in school. I ask Usha her feelings about dealing with this type of situation. Not surprisingly, she says,

I literally cried and had tears and all. I think people were trying to console me. You know, it's common every day we see, maybe you see it and you just can't bear ... I just picked her up. I picked her up. I carried her and I told her parents you come with me. Put her in school.

That she physically picked up this child and took her out of the terrible conditions in which she lived speaks to the urgency and direct nature of Usha's work, albeit emotionally difficult. She explains that this is not the only situation like this that she encountered:

It was a little difficult to teach her. It took time. We took her alone to teach her so many things. We tied one rope from one pole to another at a very far distance and made her walk. She couldn't walk and she couldn't speak properly. A six-year-old child, she could hardly speak, there was nobody to talk to her the whole day until the parents come in the evening after six. There are several cases like this, Tammy. How many can I tell you?

It took the coordination of the school, the administrator, and Usha to find this child and put her in school. Unfortunately, she passed away after leaving school. It is suspected that she ate something poisonous. She had two other sisters who were also blind and attended the school.

Usha did this work for 20 years. During that time she would regularly go to the villages. She explains what the administrators at her school felt about it:

> And even our authorities used to send me (to the villages) thinking 'You go. You'll stand as the best example. They'll see you and they'll see the way you work or talk or whatever. Then they will put their children in school.' They used to send me.

Usha's life and her accomplishments stood as an example to help change the mindset of families of other blind and visually impaired girls. Her colleagues recognized a strategic way to help convince sceptical parents to put their girls in school. Her community organizing was centred around taking children out of difficult, often violent, situations and putting them into school to be educated. They had to develop other strategies in order to earn the parents' trust so they would know that the school they would send their child to would be safe. She describes one such strategy:

> You know, I used to carry the albums and show to them school days, programmes, and children's talents, dance and singing and competitions, all that we had in photographs and children's activities. So, they saw what the children will become. We used to make up some ideas like that or take one or two girls who are very good at things – studies, and handwork and craftwork – take them along with me and show them and make them speak to the parents. I used to do so many things like that that are different. That's what I used to do: carry these photographs, albums and sometimes special children who were good at things. We would arrange a meeting with the *panchayat* at the village office. Tell them and give them information beforehand that we are coming.

Again, we see that Usha is involving the community in her recruitment efforts and using the other girls as examples to show the village leaders.

Usha's work extended to women as well. When talking about the girls who would keep in touch with her and be at her house, she mentions one girl who stayed with her. The story she tells is quite remarkable in terms of community organizing. She begins by telling me, 'Now they're all gone now. But I have one visually impaired woman with me. I rescued her from severe cyclonic weather floods.' I ask Usha to tell me more about the rescue. 'Some of her friends told me that she is suffering there. You know, and then from there we thought …' Usha stops to say, 'That's a good story, you know.' She continues:

> See there's one girl, she had three younger brothers who were very small, and one elder brother who's married. She had no parents. Okay? Then the brother and his wife were taking care of these four. This girl and three boys. And then one severe cyclone hit that year. It was all tidal wave from the sea. The whole village was drowned you can say almost. The trees fell off and it's a real misery that year.

I ask if this was a long time ago and she says 1991. She continues:

> So, at that time the government announced there is a lot of destruction. All the trees and all the rocks on the ground flew up and got stuck in the trees. It was so severe. At that time, the government announced that if any dead body was found in the water, if anyone died, give them 25,000 [rupees] to build their houses or something like that, they announced. So, taking that opportunity that brother's wife, she told him, 'What's the use of this girl? We'll just push her in the water, and we can get some money. By now she can't see and she's grown up now.' Something like that, she planned.
>
> And this girl overheard. They were all trying to sleep but they couldn't sleep. There was no house, all broken, all water, rain. So, she overheard that and she thought, 'They will really kill me', and she somehow went away from there. There was one shop, the shopkeeper's house was there, and she knew that lady before. So, she went there and she hid that night in that house. The next day one of her classmates in university, who worked as a teacher there in that village, he went and he called us and said, 'See if you don't do something. If you don't help that girl, they will kill her.' This is her situation.
>
> Before this instance he told me once about that girl and I just send some clothes and all thinking that there is nobody to take care of her. I give her this because she passed the school going age. She was 17 or something then. Then I said 'It's okay then, you bring her somehow. You bring her to me. I don't want her to be killed. In whatever state she is, just bring her to me.' He said, 'Now it's difficult. I can't bring her. It's all flooded. What to do? They'll kill her. I'm scared now.' I said 'Okay. It doesn't matter, I'll send somebody.' We sent one student from the university. 'Please, whatever you do, you go and get that girl.' And he managed to bring her. From that day, nearly seven to eight years she was with me. Nobody came to even ask about her.

In this instance, the girl's life was in real danger due to government policy intersecting with negative perceptions of disability. This girl was not valuable to her family who felt it was easy to dispose of her. That she was able to reach someone in the community at a local shop to shelter her for a night is remarkable. Just as remarkable is that she reached out to one of her classmates who was able to reach Usha. They planned to rescue the girl and, fortunately, their efforts were successful. We have a shopkeeper, a village teacher, and Usha organizing to get her out of danger. Her family did not even come to look for her. Family can have a strong influence on the lives of young girls with disabilities as can be seen by the examples of the young girls Usha was bringing to school and this young woman whose family plotted to kill her. Of the young girl's family, Usha explains:

> Her younger brothers started growing up and now they are in touch when they are coming. From that time, she is with me. From 1991 to

today she is with me. Yeah, and then she lives with me, and I taught her everything like how to be self-dependent. She is very good at it. She cooks. She learned cooking. She keeps the house very well. Even if I'm here. If Pavan or somebody goes to work at my house, she will take care of them. She's good.

That young girl is 40 now. When asked if she has had contact with her family since then, I am told that her elder brother passed away but that she goes to her younger brother's house once a year for about 10 days.

Usha says that even though she is retired now, her students have carried on teaching and promoting inclusion. Sometimes they ask for her help:

And my students who are working in schools, I go sometimes if they need me. If they want a little talk about it, about being visually impaired. They say, 'Ma'am will you please come and talk to our principal? They think we can't do anything. We won't teach', and things like that, they ask me. Then I go and talk to their principal. 'What things that they can't do? They can do everything. You give them work and see if they can't do.' Like that, you know.

Sometimes, though, parents want to use Usha as an example of a woman who did not get married in order to discourage their daughters from getting married. She tells me:

Some parents they don't want their children to get married, girls to get married after they start earning. Because they don't want their earnings to go away if she gets married and settled. So, they can't enjoy. Once, you know, there was one family that took me as example. They said, 'See your madam didn't get married. She's happily living. Why do you want to get married?'

But Usha did not even tell her own family everything she was doing because she did not want them to try to talk her out of it:

Yeah, for my retirement my sister came, and she didn't know what do or say after hearing everyone talking about me. They called her also and asked, 'Do you also want to say a few words about your sister? She did so much for the school, for the children and for us', and she just started crying. She told them, 'I didn't know what my sister was doing all these days. After hearing from you all I know. Now I'm knowing what she did all these years. She goes to school. Comes. Sometimes she says she will go to some place because some work is given to her to do. That's what we know and we didn't even know all this.'

Usha laughs and continues:

Why I didn't share with them most of my work, my outside work and all this? Because usually they say, 'No you shouldn't go there. Don't do it. Why do you stay up night?' And things like that. I'm scared when such words come out. And you know that will discourage me to do things. So, I never told them.

Usha tells me she is happy with her life, the work she has done and the connections she has made with the girls she has helped over her 20-year career.

I chose Usha's story because of the various ways she has done community organizing to help women and girls with disabilities out of violence. While doing organizing work through the establishment of organizations, Usha's approach to change through gaining access to education demonstrates that working towards change can happen in a variety of ways and through various networks.

### Education

All of the people I interviewed had access to education – in most cases, a university-level education. Usha's story most strongly emphasizes the importance of education. She herself had access to education and she went on to want the same for others. She was able to use this as a way to advocate for and improve the life circumstances of young blind and visually impaired girls in India. Five other participants identified barriers to pursuing education in school and in university, but they also describe their continued efforts to overcome those barriers. They insisted on pursing an education and actively took steps to do so, even when faced with structural, physical, attitudinal, or cultural barriers. Amal, in Yemen, tells me about going out of her home to get an education despite cultural taboos against women doing so. She emphasizes the importance of education:

> I started working in this field because it is my case and most women are isolated in their homes and negative society ... I left the house despite the bad habits and traditions that surround our society, that the departure of the woman from the house is a disgrace ... People around me looked [at me] different because of my disability but I tried to convince them to build me [up] like them and that by challenging and going out to complete my studies.

Like many participants I interviewed, Amal tells me that, after completing her own studies, she 'participated in the establishment of a society for women with disabilities and this association helped rural women to complete their studies until they became university [educated].'

Misti, Tika, and Jane, in Bangladesh, Nepal, and Kenya respectively, each identify barriers to accessing education and the extraordinary lengths to which they went to get it. The barriers included the distance between home and school, structural barriers to physically entering the schools, and the attitudes of administrators. Because of Misti's efforts, other students with disabilities were accepted into the university. She explains that (among other things, to be discussed in her story in the final theme of this section) when she learned of other women and girls not having access to education, this made her think about what she could do to change the situation and so she started an organization specifically for women with disabilities. Tika and Jane also started organizations for women with disabilities to help develop their capacities to advocate for and achieve their rights.

Two of the participants specifically do work on gender-based violence against people with disabilities at university campuses. In this sense, the educational institution is the site where transformative work on gender-based violence and disability can take place. As a reminder, Sarah is a 21-year-old student in the United States who, in addition to working at the community level, does sexual violence advocacy work on her university campus. In pursuing her education, she transferred universities because the environment at her former school was unsafe for her. Rather than leave school altogether, though, she transferred to a university in another state and is now majoring in disability studies. She continues to do advocacy on disability and gender-based violence.

Molly, in Winnipeg, describes cooperating with others to address violence on university campuses and speaks about the role that women with disabilities played. She explains, 'So, I helped pass Bill 15 in Manitoba which mandates sexual violence policies for post-secondary institutions, and this was largely done by racialized and disabled women in the community, which was really a great thing.'

Access to education for many participants was critical for their success. In turn, they have worked to advocate for other women and girls with disabilities to have the same educational opportunities and also to have a safe space to learn. Some pursued higher education in disability studies, while others worked on violence issues on their campuses. As a theme, education has figured prominently in a number of ways. As will be discussed shortly, community support has also been essential to keeping the participants feeling motivated and able to continue their advocacy work.

## Seeing oneself represented in the movement

### Charlie – Toronto, Canada

Charlie was referred to my study by another participant. For the last three years, they have been a front-line worker doing counselling and case management in Toronto. The advocacy component of their work is working with individuals who are navigating oppressive systems. They do this by being a spokesperson and collaborating with the individual to ensure that their needs are met and to help empower them to have more choices in terms of their care. They work primarily with female-identified adults who have mental health and substance-abuse challenges. I ask Charlie what brought them to this work. They tell me:

> I guess I always felt like elements of my own identity never quite shored up against the status quo and that felt like a reason to commit myself

to, to working with my people. Also, my matrilineal side of my family, they've actually all been involved in social work.

When I ask Charlie some of the challenges they face, they say they struggle with working with a gender-specific organization when their understanding of gender has expanded beyond that. They struggle with the balance between acknowledging the specific challenges that women face while also accommodating people who are non-binary or trans. They would like to see their organization work towards a more inclusive understanding of gender.

A second challenge is that the psychiatric system is built to be very oppressive and many of the women they work with have trauma related to interacting with systems including hospitals, medical systems, and psychiatric systems. Charlie shared challenges of trying to help people apply for the ODSP. They have to fit into categories in order to have basic needs met or to pay rent. This is ongoing and compounded by precarious housing conditions in Toronto. Qualifying is difficult because it is not easy to fit different life circumstances and identities into categories for the purposes of obtaining services or support.

There are issues around affordable assistive devices and wait times for accessing funding. At times, Charlie has had to advocate for patients who were being prematurely discharged from the hospital without adequate support in place at home. Other times, someone with an addiction issue is brought to hospital for something unrelated to their addiction but they are stigmatized, or if a person is intoxicated and injures themselves in the hospital, staff do not act quickly to help.

A third challenge is the toll the work has taken on Charlie. They have had to work to set boundaries for themselves, and have found that they have less time to invest in the community organizing and advocacy work that they were interested in when they were still in school. Working full time, they do not have as much energy to put into it.

In terms of what keeps them hopeful and moving forward, Charlie says it is humanity and capacity of the people they work with day-to-day, people who are operating in a world that isn't built for them. To be able to find humour, connection, and a sense of hope while trusting Charlie enough to share their struggles with them even though Charlie is in a position of power. Sometimes it's the small acts, liking having a coffee at a coffee shop with someone who just needs to talk.

### Seeing oneself in the work

This theme is linked to the next theme, of wanting a better situation for others, but I will discuss them separately. In Charlie's case, the motivation to do this work was not seeing themself represented in the work. Charlie does not go into detail about what this means in terms of their own experience, but what is important is that it leads to a desire to change the system. Six other participants refer to their own experience with disability and violence when asked how they became involved in this work. The experiences range from being institutionalized to experiencing negative perceptions within the community and wanting to change that. One participant describes how doing this work has a healing aspect for them. Usha describes using her experience as a blind woman to help educate parents of children who are blind or low vision about what they are capable of. She is open about using her own successes as an example for others.

## Wanting a better situation for others

### Molly – Manitoba, Canada

Molly responded to my call for participants through a social media post. Molly is a 23-year-old student in Manitoba who has been doing disability advocacy work for six years. She is the co-chair of Sexuality and Disability Manitoba, an organization that works on representation in the media and prioritizes having robust conversations about sexuality and disability without solely focusing on sexual violence, instead highlighting also the right to have sexual relationships. She has done self-advocacy work related to consent culture legislation on campuses. She, along with largely racialized women and other disabled women, helped pass Bill 15, The Sexual Violence Awareness and Prevention Act (Advanced Education Administration Act and Private Vocational Institutions Act)[1]. Molly is also the National Disability Justice Commissioner for the Canadian Federation of Students in Winnipeg. She has been doing specific work on gender-based violence in the disability community for four years. When I ask what brought her to this work, she tells me that it is a consequence of being assaulted and then forcibly institution-alized for coming forward about her assault.

Molly talks about being catcalled as a woman with a disability. She recalls feeling at first like she just had bad luck, but then realizing it was more than that. She says:

> Being revictimized so many times and never having a break from that and people always being like, 'What is it about you that makes this always happen for so long?' I was just like, 'I don't know. I just have bad luck.' But I don't have bad luck. I'm just disabled, and that's what happens. Even the concept of people thinking that it's bad luck is really what started it for me, and then also just a lack of conversation.

Molly says that, despite the history of disability rights advocacy in Winnipeg, the disability community is small and still run by the same people, primarily men. She says the movement currently does not make space for gender non-conforming people or younger people. She expresses the importance of having a seat at the table as someone experiencing ongoing victimization yet continuously working against it. Of her experience within the disability movement, she says, 'So, it's just been me yelling at men a lot.' Even when she is invited to speak on panels about sexual violence, it is still a surprise to her that a woman with disability is included.

I ask Molly what challenges she faces doing her advocacy. She says exhaustion is a big one. She gives the example of being assaulted while she was in the middle of a case for being stalked. She says it's also hard when there are so many communities that rally together and disability is always left out of the conversation. Like Sarah, Molly mentions the hate crimes that people with disabilities experience. But this does not get attention. About this she says, 'I think it's this lack of consciousness about us existing.'

In thinking about the context where Molly lives and works, she says Manitoba is home to the last two institutions in Canada: they are living with the terrible history of institutionalization, eugenics, and sterilization of people with disabilities. She says that it does not matter how much experience you have with violence, you still don't qualify to have a seat at the table and, for Molly, this is exhausting. Additionally, with so many issues affecting people with disabilities, there are competing priorities and the hardest issues get neglected.

The policy landscape is also challenging. Governments have made financial decisions to focus on security in psychiatric institutions instead of rehabilitation. This only increases the unnecessary policing of people with disabilities.

The interview took place around the time of the #MeToo Movement[2] and Molly raises the concern that women with disabilities have been left out. There is violence perpetrated by service providers, for example, and if the abuse is reported, the person still relies on the same people day-to-day. She expresses a feeling of a growing divide in the #MeToo movement because things are not really improving for disabled women.

She is angry about women with disabilities being abused, infantilized, and hyper-medicalized. She tells me that it's okay to be angry at the system and to be angry at the people who are part of the system. She says progress is slow and sometimes painful.

When I ask Molly what keeps her going, she says that it is the networks of care she has created with other disabled people, especially other queer disabled people. Of this support she says:

> It's life affirming because we all share these experiences that are horrible and so, yeah, that one time you enter a room and there's another young disabled person using a cane and you both are so excited because you never get to see another person in the room. It's those moments where you finally get to see another person and then you cry.

Molly expresses the love she has for her disability community and all of the women with disabilities from the past whom she has not been able to meet. She places emphasis on this history because the feminist movement in Canada has historically disenfranchised disabled women but, she says, 'We survive and move forward. I just love my young disabled people and disabled women, queer disabled folks.' She tells me about her work around sex and disability in Manitoba and how the group she works with has grown from three to two hundred. She says it's nice to have the space to have the conversations. Of her motivations, she says that she does this work because she does not want other people to experience the same abuse that she faces in her advocacy work. She says, 'I would rather take the brunt than someone else because ... I can continue.'

### Wanting a better situation for others

Molly's story demonstrates a sense of community, her need to act out of necessity, and not wanting others to experience the same abuse and violence. Many participants, when asked why they do the work they do, say it is because they want a better situation and outcomes for others. They want to establish supports for women, girls, and trans people with disabilities who experience various forms of violence.

When I ask Amal about what is rewarding in her work, she says it is the growing number of women with disabilities in society, something that she wanted when she began her work. Fran expresses a similar hope for things getting better, 'I don't think that it will be in my lifetime, but I really want to believe that we are going to get to a place where we will no longer tolerate violence against women.' Sometimes this motivation is paired with feelings of anger about gender-based violence in the disability community, as we saw with Sarah earlier, but when participants discuss their feelings of anger, it is framed as a motivation to create change.

Several participants expressed feeling the need to do something almost as if it is not a choice but rather a drive. Sarah says that doing the work helps with feelings of anger:

> If I don't do something that doesn't mean it will stop happening ... All this stuff is going to keep happening no matter what. I feel like it's kind of my responsibility to at least try to make it a little bit better. It's kind of like that quote, 'If not me, who?' I think that that's really important, and I think that this is also how you keep hopeful.

Keegan engages in community events in Toronto such as Take Back the Night. Like Sarah, when asked about their work, Keegan directly expressed a feeling of 'I can't not do this.' For Keegan, getting into activism has been a way to reclaim themself after leaving an abusive relationship. Empowerment, without it being called such, appears to be a powerful motivator. When Charlie did not see elements of their identity represented in the support systems, they wanted to get involved. They wanted to become an advocate alongside those who do not often have a voice.

When asked what brought her to this work, Patricia tells me that she identifies as a psychiatric survivor and, reflecting on her experience being hospitalized, she felt there must be a better way to do things, a better way to work with people. Patricia explains her solution to not wanting others to feel the way she did was to pursue education. She reflects on encountering helpful and supportive individuals within a system that is not designed to be supportive, and explains how this led to her studying in an effort to create a better situation for others. Jane expresses a similar desire to think about ways to do things differently because, as a woman with a disability, she was always told what she couldn't do. She wants better for others. This is highlighted in Jane's story in the next section.

It has become clear that the themes that have emerged are interconnected in various ways. Education is raised as a solution to wanting a better situation for others, for example. In much the same way that the participants want better for others, they were also motivated by raising awareness about women with disabilities experiencing violence.

## Raised awareness

### Jane – Nairobi, Kenya

I first met Jane while working at the Coady International Institute in 2014, when she was a participant in the Diploma in Development Leadership programme. Jane responded to my call for participants via social media. Jane is a woman with a physical disability who grew up and works in Kenya. When I asked Jane why she works on issues of violence, I gained insight to some of the challenges she faced growing up with a disability. She speaks about societal norms and challenges to getting an education, an issue that has come up throughout this study:

> I am a woman with a disability, physical disability, so I could relate it to my life when I was growing up. How I was in the community. I was never accepted fully in the community because when it comes to issues of marriage, relationships, no one wants to get a woman with disability. Nobody wants to marry a woman with a disability. And even when I went through the education system … no inclusivity of those with special educational needs. I had really to struggle through the system. I didn't go to a special school; I went to an ordinary school. And having a physical disability and you have to go several floors, through stairs, going up, going down. It was stress and even after school. Whatever I wanted to be in life, I wanted to be a nurse. I couldn't do that because people would see my disability before me and all they could do is say that I can't do it.

Like many of the participants in my study, Jane refers to the motivation gained from going through her own challenges and the desire to create a better situation for women with disabilities who come after her. The association of disability with inability is highlighted by Jane. She expresses a desire to work against that perception:

> So, we live in a world that disability is related with what you can't do. People never see what you can do. So that also prompted me to think

about that as a programme director. There are others who have been through the same, who have gone through the same and something needs to be done around that.

Jane is the executive director of an organization for women with disabilities called Women Challenged to Challenge. One of their programmes focuses specifically on violence against women. She explains:

One of our programmes that we carry out is elimination of all forms of violence against women and this is because women are violated, and we needed to do something in order to be able to address this. So, we did research at the community level to be able to understand what women go through. What are these forms of violence experienced? We came to learn that, despite our new constitution that prohibits discrimination at all levels, women with disability are still experiencing that. They are not fully included in development programmes. Even in the government programme.

Government commitment is a challenge that comes out of almost all of the interviews for this study. Across contexts, government policy and commitment to addressing violence against women with disabilities are raised as concerns.

Jane also talks about the women's movement in her country and her feeling that it is not inclusive of women with disabilities. This was a driving force for Jane and her organization to start a programme on violence against women with disabilities:

And you know, the women's rights movement, when they are talking of equality, they forget women with disabilities. We have other needs that they don't have, and our issues would be different ... They need to be addressed and they need to be highlighted. It is only those who know them who could do that. So, we felt even left out by the women's rights movement. So that's how we started the programme.

Like many other participants in this study, Jane raises concerns about how family influence and access to education affect violence against women with disabilities:

At the family level, they fear they are left out. Issues [are] access to services, access to information, and access even to education. We still have a big number of girls who are still not accessing education despite that there is free primary education.

As part of their work, her organization conducted research in 10 different counties in Kenya. She found there were similar issues across counties:

Actually, wherever we went, the issues were the same and issues of sexual abuse were highly highlighted. That women and girls with disabilities experience sexual abuse, rape, defilement – and the worse part of it is that these cases go unreported.

I ask Jane about the challenges of doing work on violence towards women and girls with disabilities. She mentions societal perceptions and access to justice as two key issues:

> The challenge is people's perception still, yeah, around disability, they have not changed. And the change I wanted is something that takes time to do. Another challenge is our systems. Especially justice. How are they? They are constructed in a way that there are a lot of barriers that one would face to access justice.

Her solution is community organizing and empowerment where, again, education becomes key:

> So that is one of the key challenges that we face. Again, women with disabilities in most of the counties they are not really organized so we have to organize them ... The capacity starts from the scratch and then even before [that] we train them on how to advocate for their rights. How to do the advocacy work. We have to expand their capacity. Some of them are not well educated, they have no education. So, again, under-standing some of these issues, being able to carry out the project. It is quite a challenge.

At a systems level, inclusion of women with disabilities and their issues in the community is a hurdle:

> ... one of the challenges is that even you go to the community level and you find different people doing different things in terms of development ... but they are not inclusive. Even when leaders come to us to promote during elections, they forget about that and any programme they have, it's never inclusive.

She goes on to say that this challenge is reflected at the international level as well, and she has worked to change that:

> And, so, I could say again that is another challenge, a lack of inclusivity even at the international level. If you look at the status of women, the CEDAW, Convention on the Elimination of all forms of Discrimination against Women, is that they have never paid attention to what goes around women with disabilities until last year when they were able to compare that. We wrote a report on the status of women with disabilities in Kenya. So, the writing part of it is what I did. I've been able to change, right? Those with disabilities, those without, have come to know, yes? We have been including these people and we cannot be called developers if there is a section of people we are leaving out.

Jane discusses how the inclusion of women with disabilities in politics is challenging: even if they are accepted as candidates, they also have to have the capacity to run a campaign. She tells me about another form of community organizing, encouraging women with disabilities to run for elections:

> During our national election, we encouraged several women with disabilities to give themselves for elected position, which they did. Although they were not elected. We had only about two or three who were elected. Others did not make it. But that is quite a milestone, given that they attempted to do that. They tried doing it. Which means too that they will be open now. They've gotten experience to do a campaign. We have more than those three now being elected.

I wanted to know what keeps Jane going amidst these challenges. Like many other participants in the study, she is hopeful about change and this change affects her too. In fact, she feels empowered:

> The biggest reward is that I have been able to bring change in the lives of women with disabilities and even mine. I feel stronger and stronger every day that people can't be able to discriminate against me because I am a woman, because I have a disability. I am able to tell when my rights have been violated.

Jane has a drive to keep going:

> The different skills that I've gotten in the process keeps me going. And then I remember the values that I got at Coady International Institute when we were doing the community development. And, as a leader, you don't give up. So, there's that spirit in me that doesn't want to give up. And even when little changes happen, that really motivates, and if we can change one percent why not go even to five percent? So, still, that women with disabilities, when they're enlightened, they're able to now demand for their space. That keeps me going.

Jane's story highlights the experiences many advocates face in addressing their own barriers as well as societal, structural, and environmental barriers. Jane's drive to do this work is a mixture of wanting a better situation for others and seeing changes, however small, as motivation to keep moving forward.

### Raised awareness

Jane's story highlights a continued effort on her part to raise awareness about the rights of women and girls with disabilities. This effort is directed towards society, families, government, and even women with disabilities themselves. In terms of outcomes, being able to raise the profile of women with disabilities and their concerns about violence in communities, families, and at the government level is important.

Social media is another avenue to raise awareness. Keegan talks about their efforts: 'I do a good deal of social media sharing and articles around trauma and women and also queer and trans folks and how our lives intersect with violence.' Others work through organizations to raise awareness. Usha worked through her school to help make families aware of their blind or visually impaired daughter's capacity to attend school. She says:

> They are not aware of schools and all. No? There are children in villages. The parents are not aware and here we don't conduct much awareness programmes for them. To know where the school is. What is their future? Where they have to go. Whom to meet. They won't know all that. That's part of our study. We have to do that, actually. To explain everything and to show them what it is.

Fran speaks about her earlier career and the work she did to raise awareness about gender-based violence in the disability community by becoming a voice within the women's movement:

> My earlier days with the DisAbled Women's Network was really the opportunity for me to take what I was learning both from other women that were doing this work with DAWN and also the work that came out of that research. [It was] being at the table with other researchers and activists that weren't necessarily looking at disability within the context of gender-based violence but had allowed me to squeeze in to be part of the conversations.

Misti gives an example of raising awareness about legal rights for women with disabilities in Bangladesh so they and their families understand how to go to the police or through the court process:" So, from our organization we are trying to raise more awareness to stop violence against women with disabilities. We published a book on how to get access to justice."

Tika speaks about similar work to Misti's in raising awareness about legal rights through her organization. She says, 'We're able to raise awareness among women with disabilities and other communities and their families. Now, at least when they face violence, then they connect with us. They share their problem and we provide the support there.'

For Sarah, raised awareness is indicated through people getting angry and passionate about issues. She says:

> I think that there are more people who are fighting against things like abusive therapies. But now people who are in favour of them are fighting back even harder.

Sarah explains that if people push back against her work, she sees it as a sign of progress because it shows that they are having an impact.

Molly talks about the reactions she gets when she is bringing attention to gender-based violence and disability:

> I think continuously hearing people being like, 'Oh this is interesting. This is the first I'm hearing about this, and you've taught me so much.' I guess I'm the first person saying these things, which is shocking to me and a bit offensive. How am I the first person telling you this? But, I guess,

just as long as people are willing to challenge their ongoing perceptions of their understanding of gender-based violence, it's important.

Awareness among women with disabilities and their families is also a sign of progress for Amal in Yemen. When I ask her what keeps her hopeful, she responds with, 'My goal is coming true and some people in our society are also aware of the importance of the rights of women with disabilities.' She references the establishment of many organizations in her country that are concerned with women's issues and women with disabilities, in particular.

When asked about changes in the nature of her work over time, Elizabeth in Ghana talks about how the women she works with have a raised awareness about their rights and they have a system in place to report rights violations:

> Now I would say it has changed and it's changing gradually because, as I indicated, now that persons with disabilities are aware of their rights, they are not hiding violation of their rights and, again, we've also put systems in place where they can confide. With the increase in technology and media they are also able to throw light on issues that have been hidden, or would have been hidden, in the dark in the communities.

She further speaks of the importance of awareness raising about legislation so they are prepared to demand for their rights:

> All this capacity building that we do for them in the community is just to let them be aware of who they are, irrespective of being visually impaired, and then taking advantage of legislations available to them.

Karen, in Australia, expresses similar sentiments:

> I've seen more women with disabilities in leadership positions and there's more support for women with disabilities being able to accept leadership positions. So, for example, in Australia we have a lot of women with disabilities within the disability community that are really holding their own and demonstrating a lot of leadership in this space and talking out about women's issues and violence and sterilization … There was a new article brought out about how the National Disability Insurance scheme seems to be advantaging men a lot more than women so we're addressing that now.

Awareness raising can as easily be tied to the rights challenges addressed in the last chapter as it can to the next theme: community organizing and support.

## Community organizing and support

### Tika – Kathmandu, Nepal

I met Tika in Nepal and conducted the first part of our interview in Kathmandu. Due to scheduling, we arranged to finish the interview remotely once I returned to Toronto. Tika does extensive work on gender equality and disability, from lobbying and networking to advocacy and coordination of disability rights work. Priorities for Tika also include addressing laws and policies so that they are disability friendly for women, and helping other women with disabilities access justice when experiencing violence. Tika who had polio as a child was discouraged from going out of her house to go to school. She tells me about being isolated and having difficulty making friends. She says:

> I felt very alone and I always felt very discriminated against and disturbed … And along with this, many times I felt sexual harassment. When I show respect to teacher, other friends and other people – men – they try to exploit that. They try to always tease me and focus on sexuality.

After school, Tika joined an organization for people with disabilities in Nepal but noticed there were very few women involved. Like some of the other participants in this study, Tika took this as a motivation to start an organization. She and other women with disabilities began networking:

> I took training and I took other kinds of initiations, but along with that [I was in a] very insecure situation at that time. When I got job as a computer operator, at that time, that institution also was not too focused on disability. They are a construction company and there were many engineers working there. They try to exploit me every time. When I connected to men they also tried to exploit [me] and they offered sex and other things. I really was upset and slowly, slowly I felt very disturbed, upset. I tried to find other friends and then tried to share my experience. I felt very insecure at that time, you know? And other ladies, other colleagues they also share when I met them. They also share the same similar kind of history. And then we decided to start this Nepal Disabled Women Association.

Before starting the organization, Tika explains that she was not taken seriously by men in the disability movement in Nepal:

> Men always thought that they were very much higher people. They are talented they thought. Women they are always backward, they thought. 'They are not educated. They don't plan anything. They cannot do anything.' And then I tried to crush that thing. No, we want to do. We want to show positivity. We want equal contribution within the movement. But nobody listens to my voice at that time. Very few programmes were organized at that time, and I tried to participate in the programme but nobody invited me. Just they are using rallies and, demonstrations (which is) very difficult work in the street. We were demanding our rights together and we were very much shouting … But when they organized the training, they forgot our needs, our participation. And then I felt, 'Oh they see I'm a woman and they try gender discrimination.' … Many women with disabilities can come even slowly.

Slowly people know about my work, my organization's work, Nepal Disabled Women's Association.

After she had started the organization, women came together and began telling similar stories of discrimination and violence. Many women came to them because they were not being supported by their family. Tika tells me what their organization did to help and explains that, from the beginning, networking with the women with disabilities was very important:

But we are very hopeful, and we started networking among women with disabilities. Then we tried to encourage each other, and we tried to establish the platform for sharing. Slowly, we raised money for each person. We tried to explain our objectives; why we are collecting the money, why we are doing the income generating activities, and we thought we [should] develop a concept for the support. If we provide the support to victims of violence, women with disabilities, especially rape victims, and we establish the support, then we will find other problems.

Tika tells me about some of the issues the women had to learn how to manage, particularly in the first year of establishing their organization:

From the beginning, I think after establishing the organization, after four years we were just doing capacity building: how to do advocacy, how to identify the issues, who are our stakeholders? How to make connections with women with disabilities and their family, who are the rights activists? Who are the rights persons? Many things we prepared during one year ... And then how to establish the organization: how to make money, how to run the activities, how to collect the money, how to make sustainable programmes, how to connect to another agency, how to prepare report, what is the concept note? What is the DPO proposal?

So many things I learned, and capacity building for ourselves during one year. During that one year we established the organization, we prepared a brochure, we prepared our bylaws, consultation, organizing, and membership ... And then I think, after that four years, we just focused on capacity ... increased membership and capacity building of women with disabilities: starting the self-help groups, starting the network. We conducted a few activities like leadership training, advocacy training ... And we received many violence against women with disabilities cases. Then we started to work on access to justice and a campaign to remove the violence against women with disabilities.

For Tika, access to justice is very important. Her organization works with women to register their cases and prepare them for court. Her organization went so far as to organize a safe house for women who were victims of violence:

We established a home. Initially, we just rented a house. There is one house. We increased slowly, slowly and we rented one building, a five-row building, and we provided for seventeen women with disabilities at one time. Now we construct a new building, our own building, and we target, I hope we provide for 100 women with disabilities. Those who are victims and those who were raped. We are planning for that. We have one building now, and not only in Kathmandu, but also in eastern region, one district, to focus at the community level.

Watching the organization grow, not just in size but also in scope, has been among the rewards for Tika:

We just started from seven women with disabilities. We are very scarce ... and we started from Kathmandu, the capital city, but now we go all over the country. That is the greatest achievement. And initially very few DPOs were there and women with disabilities organizations, [there was] only our Nepal Disabled Women's Association. Now, we have almost 16 women with disabilities organizations working at the national and community level, district level ...

We should contribute to many stakeholder organizations and human rights organizations and other big networks – disability work, violence against women, human rights, trafficking, STDs, gender and many things under our network .... Many women with disabilities, rape victims, and domestic violence victims and other women with disabilities, they were able to report the case, register the case, and go to court. We received not many, but a few. We got justice, you know?

Tika has worked extensively at the national and international level as well serving on an advisory committee for UN Women. She has focused her attention on the Nepal government on policy changes related to reproductive health, medical care, and disability rights for women.

Tika's hope is that more and more women with disabilities will become empowered. Over time, she has seen issues of violence against women with disabilities raised more in the media and parents become more aware of the issues. However, the courts are not yet accessible to women with disabilities. She also says that, while things like education, health or participation are easier for people to talk about, there is still resistance to addressing violence:

But, if I talk about violence against women with disabilities, like the many rape cases that we are receiving .... men, those who have already contributed, very strong leaders, they always keep silent, you know? That is very challenging. They thought, 'That is not my responsibility. That is your responsibility, Tika because you are long time contributing for that. You are a leader in this thing.' You know? That is a big challenge with our team.

She still faces the challenge that women's organizations do not feel they have the capacity to deal with disability issues and, at the same time, disability organizations expect women's organizations to deal specifically with those issues. Going forward, she tells me, 'We still have to work on [issues affecting] women with disabilities in our network for the sensitization awareness, advocacy, capacity building, so I'm thinking about that. We have to do it together.'

### Community organizing and support

I chose Tika's story to highlight community organizing and support because she identifies several challenges that she and her organization experienced while they were establishing the organization and describes the strategies they used. She also describes feeling supported by others during this process. Four of the participants I interviewed started organizations specifically for women with disabilities. Misti tells me that her organization developed through a network of women with disabilities with a shared vision of addressing the specific concerns of women with disabilities that were neglected by the disability movement. She describes various ways she and her organization reached out to women with disabilities to get them involved. For example, they networked with the Bangladesh National Women Lawyer Association so that when women with disabilities reached out to Misti's organization about rights violations or abuse, they would have a resource to refer them to. Community organizing can happen within networks of women with disabilities, but it can also bring in other organizations who can offer support.

Some of the participants speak about the support they feel from other people in the movement when they engage in anti-violence work. For some, self-healing takes place when advocating for others. Sarah addresses her feelings of anger by following her need to act. In helping others, she feels a sense of healing of her own trauma:

> I think that there's kind of the dual motivation. So, one is just anger and there's some things where it's just like, 'I can't not do something.' Then also, I really believe in this healing through helping. A lot of times my parents didn't want me to do this work because they're like, 'It's so emotionally taxing,' and it is. And sometimes it does create problems for me emotionally, especially as someone with PTSD from this type of violence. But I think that, in a way, by helping others I'm kind of also helping myself. And I think that, for me, it's always been easier for me to stick up and advocate for other people than for myself. But this has helped me do that better because I feel like if I'm fighting for other survivors, I'm also fighting for myself.

She says that doing this work helps give her a sense of control and like she is doing her part. Sarah also says that, while some people resist the work she is doing (via public posts on Facebook, for example) the support she gets from the community helps her know that there are people behind her. Keegan tells me something similar: 'I left an abusive relationship around that time. And getting back into activist spaces has been part of reclaiming myself and coming back to myself. And so, it feels like home.' They go on to say, 'Activism for me is that meaning-making, it's building community in response to isolation, it's empowering which counteracts feeling powerless. It's the medicine and, yeah, I need it.'

There is humanity involved in this work that keeps people going and a sense that this could be lonely and isolating work were it not for the community support participants feel. Charlie, in Toronto, is a support worker – a job that can be emotionally taxing – but, when asked what keeps them motivated, they say:

> It's just the huge amount of humanity that I get to bump up against day-to-day and the extraordinary capacity of people who are literally plugging away day after day in a world that's not built for them. Kind of like against all odds … [they are] able to find humour and connection and their own senses of hope, and [they] trust me enough to share that with me even though I'm in a position where they have every reason not to trust me. I'm in a position of power in a lot of ways, so I think that is really what has kept me going so far and continues to. I like to, you know, just be able to go to Tim Horton's and have a coffee and drink it in the rain with someone who's just needing to chat … I like being in solidarity with people in that way.

Charlie feels empowered through being able to support people who are experiencing violence. Molly emphasizes the importance of meeting other people to relate to as a motivator for continuing the work (see Molly's story on page 130):

> I think also those networks of care that you create with other disabled folks and it's like the only thing that keeps me going because I don't know what I'd do without other disabled people, especially queer disabled people, in my life.

After she has explained the structural issues that make it hard to advocate, I ask Patricia in Toronto what keeps her hopeful. She tells me that, by working together, people realize they have the answers within themselves. She says:

> People coming together, and supporting each other, and realizing that they have the answer in themselves, or with each other just talking, like just collaborating. That's where the unfolding of, I wouldn't so much say solutions, not really the right word, but ways of moving toward a direction that they want to go. Ways of moving towards a preferred future. The unfolding of that comes out in the community when people are creating together and ways that people don't even expect. That's where the magic is, I think. This is where it's important.

Jane, in Kenya, describes the impact that community organizing has had in her life. What has been most rewarding for Jane is noted in her story, above, but bears repeating here: 'The biggest reward is that I have been able to bring change in the lives of women with disabilities and even mine, that I feel stronger and stronger every day.'

If we think back to Usha's story, there are several instances of community organizing. Take, for instance, the young girl who feared being murdered by her family so they could get compensation for her death: that young woman reached out to someone in the community who reached out to Usha. That Usha had networks she could call upon to help the young woman reach safety is a powerful expression of community organizing. Then there is the community outreach and working with local councils to encourage families to allow their children to go to school. And there is the house that Usha bought to provide a living space for the young girls to live while they studied.

All of these are examples of community organizing in support of women and trans people with disabilities experiencing violence. Cooperation and support, then, is helpful for many of the participants, but they recognize that this is powerful for the women they work with as well. The participants describe a collective empowerment that moves people towards common interests and goals. These women and trans people emphasize working together as a way to keep them going in spaces that are emotionally tense at times.

## Advocacy

### Misti – Dhaka, Bangladesh

Misti was born and raised 300 kilometres outside of Dhaka, Bangladesh. She acquired a spinal cord injury after falling from a rooftop when she was 14 years old. After spending one and a half years in rehabilitation, Misti returned home and pursued her schooling. She was accepted to do a bachelor's degree, but the university refused to let her attend because of her disability. She then did a fast-track degree and was admitted to college to do a master's in accounting. She tells me that they again tried to deny her admission but, out of necessity, she advocated for herself and worked to prove that she was capable:

> College tried to deny me the first time then I take a challenge and see myself as self-advocate and I talk with the principal of that college. I said that 'If you give me one chance to go to class in your college then one week later you can find out that I am talented or not and you can side with me. If I do not get your education successfully then I will go out without any question.' Then the principal became very angry and said, 'Why do you say that seven days is enough for just ensuring your talent?' I said that, 'No Sir, there is a system. You can take the class test and if I do good then you can give me the chance to continue my study.' Then the teacher said, 'Okay let's see what happen.' Then they

give me chance to take the class. Six classes I attended in the college, and I took three plus tests and I got first position, so high marks. So, then our principal said, 'Okay, you will be permanently a student at my college.' And I continued my studies.

The college appeared to have assumed that because she had a disability Misti would not be capable academically. She says that the teachers were very happy with her performance and declared that they would allow other students with disabilities entry to the college.

Then Misti began working towards starting her career. She got an interview with an organization, but the executive director questioned her on very intimate aspects of how she would manage her personal care with a spinal cord injury. She tells me she was very disheartened to be questioned about such personal things and that this created a challenge for her:

> So, he just make a caution on my personal management, so I was so much disheartened and said that 'It is my personal things and I manage myself and come with this disease.' I got this disability in 1992 and at that time it was over 2000 so already I was over eight years with my disability, but no organization gave me the chance to work with them.

Misti had been keen on advocacy and activism since her time at university and this transferred over to her work. She got a job with a disability organization as a receptionist but pursued additional work with the organization: advocating with the Social Welfare Ministry in Bangladesh to make the entrance to their building accessible. She met with the Ministry and advocated for a ramp to be installed outside and an accessible washroom inside. This resulted in the first ramp being added to a Ministry building in Bangladesh.

Misti tells me that women with disabilities face abuse outside and inside the home. She is currently the Executive Director of Women with Disabilities Development Foundation. She founded this organization in 2007 after seeing that there were basically no services for women with disabilities in Bangladesh. Access to justice is a major concern for Misti and her organization. Much of her work now centres on helping women and girls access legal resources. She explains:

> We have different cases in our hands. Like, at the moment, we're now seeing five cases in different districts of Bangladesh, not in Dhaka, outside of Dhaka. Most of the cases we see the women and girls they are living, the victim girls are living in the very hard, poor families. So, they have no choice to go to court, no choice to talk with the parents, to talk with the lawyers or the organizations about how they get justice. But even some girls and women with disabilities does not understand what is justice because they have intellectual disabilities. So, we are trying to talk with the parents and talk with the legal aid organizations. They have to give priority on the justice of these victim girls.

She tells me that often they do not get justice because the families are poor and the perpetrators are rich. The challenges to doing advocacy work are many:

> When we talk about the justice for the girl victims and women with disabilities there are more than three components standing against our voice. First, there is no policy. There is no outreach on how to provide the support to the victim in the court. Second, the girls with disabilities or victims with disabilities they have no choice to talk with the parents or the legal aid organization. Third, the parents' economical condition is not so good to continue the procedures because this is a long procedure. So, this is the third thing and it is very challenging. And fourth is our organization, our organization is a very small organization. We have very few manpower. We could not continue our effort through the legal aid organization and the families very frequently. That is the challenge to do that, but we do advocacy with the government to incorporate the issues in our act.

So organizational capacity is a concern. They do what they can with the legal aid organization and working with families, but they face many challenges. Like some of the other participants, Misti tells me about organizational and structural challenges that affect her work, especially as a small organization:

> ... sometimes we have the very will and the force that we want to do something, but the development partner, they think that ... 'If we support the big organization, they will do more things.' But, basically, the small organization, they do hard things and best things so the development worker never sees that support should go to small organizations who will utilize most of the money for the benefit of the people.

When I asked Misti why she does the work that she does, she too mentions the lack of representation of women with disabilities and her desire to fill the gap. Like many of the participants in this study, Misti also saw that a lot of men with disabilities were in the movement but they were not making space for women and their issues. Interestingly, she says that the women who were involved were not taking their commitments seriously. She explains:

> Okay, when I started my work in DPOs, at that time I saw that there were many DPOs and NGOs. Only DPOs are interested to recruit men with disabilities. I started a job in a DPO where a large number of staff are men with disabilities and very few there are women with disabilities. In the management committee of the organization, there are few women with disabilities. But the very few women with disabilities, they are very attentive, they always bring great work, but there is no recognition. There is the executive committee and also the general committee; one third of the members in the executive and general committee are

women with disabilities, but they don't have any leadership programme or initiatives to build their leadership capacity. So, they do not give any suggestion. They do not make any decision about how to improve the organizational capacity or raise their voice for the important things or benefit of women and girls with disabilities. I see there are different projects of different organizations, not only this organization, but also other organizations who are working for people with disabilities. They have no activity for the girls and women with disabilities. Like education, they have education support or education programme for the child with disabilities, but they never prioritize women with disabilities, girls with disabilities. So, the education level is very low for girls and women with disabilities. These things basically make me think about how to change the situation.

The establishment of the Women with Disabilities Development Foundation is itself a clear example of community organizing. Misti explains how she worked to establish the organization:

So, I talked to different women with disabilities who are working in different organizations, inside of my organization, and I have some colleagues they work in other places – non-disabled people's organizations and my previous organization – to organize a national seminar on the engagement of women with disabilities in the development process. It was my one strategy to find out the correct information for the organization to change their mindset. So, they conduct a seminar. They were very happy because this type of seminar they never organized before. They organize different events, but they do not think about the women with disabilities engagement in the development process. That was a three-day seminar. So, I invite 100 women with disabilities from different places of the country. So, they come to Dhaka and they talked about their experience, shared their experience and the same things to what I feel in Dhaka.

So, at that time, I requested my organization to make a network among the women with disabilities across the country, but they say, 'No it is not needed, a network. You can make a meeting in different districts and you can coordinate from that.' So, I was disheartened at that time, but I never show them that I am disappointed. I talk with another colleague, Shirin. She is also the country coordinator at Disability Rights Promotion International. She is working in disabled people's organizations. She has long experience. Now she is the president of South Asian Disability Forum, it is south Asian countries. And another colleague, Masuma, she also is very talented woman. Both have visual impairment. So, we three women are just talking and then we said, 'Yes we should have a platform. Yes, we need a platform then we can raise our voice, we can work independently.' So, gradually we are thinking to do this for three years and then we take initiation in 2007.

Misti networked with associations and journalists to advocate for inclusion:

> There should be some strong organization where they can open their heart, where they can say everything they need. So, we start to work on violence against women with disabilities, we gather the information through the newspaper and after that we see there are very few news stories on violence against girls and women with disabilities and what is happening regularly in our society. So, we think that we have to work on this in a different aspect. Like, we have to network with the journalist, we have to network with the legal aid organization, we have to network with the lawyer association, we have to advocate government to have some strong policy and act to prevent the violence against women with disabilities. So, we started this way.

Perhaps most interestingly, when I ask Misti about what keeps her motivated to do this work, given all that she has faced, she gives emphasis and importance to her father's support. So, family context is important here. Her father did not want her to be treated differently because she acquired a disability:

> I do not have disability from my birth. I got spinal cord injured at the start of my life. When I become disabled, from this time I see there is difference in my life, what is disability? What is not disability? So, in my family I am very lucky that my father and mother both are educated. My father always wanted that I will be someone who is never dominated by others, who always keeps her head up, not down. That is the thing my father has said, and my father loved me so much. Inside I wished to do always. After my disability, I never accept people who will help me in my daily life. Like cleaning my room or just organizing my study table or my room. I never allow my mother or my sister-in-law to organize my clothes, organize my books or clean my room. I appreciated my father. My father said that, 'God has a mission so you become disabled. So, we have to remove some barriers and specific barriers faced by women with disabilities, and we have to give more strong emphasis to the girls with intellectual disabilities because they never understand what are the rights for themselves, or they never think that this is the life or what should be the life, in their life.' So, my father was the motivator of me.

She tells me of the differences between herself and her brother who also has a disability. She explains how things are different for her because she is a woman and also because she is a wheelchair user, whereas her brother is a man with some mobility due to his type of polio:

> When I got disabled, at that time one of my brothers is also disabled. He is polio victimized. He completed his master's in economics at Jhangir Nagar University, Dhaka. He has polio so he has some mobility

so he can go in the society everywhere he wants to. But, as a woman, as a spinal cord injured person, as a different type of disability – he and me are in the same category, physical disability. But due to my womanhood, due to my spinal cord injury – to my limited mobility – I am different than him. So, I think that the woman, we are always deprived from the different type of things. My brother has developed his family. He has three children. He has a very excellent wife. But I am single. Like that type of things. We both are highly educated, complete master's, having job, same talent though we are different due to social acceptance.

She talks about how her experience has motivated her to make change:

This is the things I always feel. That's why I keep continuing my work. And we have a very strong fight with some leader with disabilities who are men to keep out our leadership of this organization. They tried, they said they will be the head of the organization and we will be the staff, or like this, we will always obey them. But we do not put down our head. We said that no, this is our organization, women's organization, so we will do everything. We will not take any advice from the leaders with disabilities who are men. We take advice from you if we feel that it is good for the women.

Misti had to be clear that she did not need men to lead their organization that was established by women with disabilities. She speaks about working directly with girls and women with disabilities, so I ask her what she tells them when they are facing challenges. She talks about the power within, and the ways in which self-perception can impact a person's experience:

Just try to talk with the girls and women with disabilities to see inside, first. What is inside is much stronger than outside because outside – the environment, the family members, the friends, the community people – they are struggling, or things are harder for them. But inside that is absolutely their own. So, inside there is some power, so even you won't see inside. Get the power and ignore the outside barriers. If inside is not powerful, then people could not go far. Because we have one example in the world, the president come from the very poor family. Okay, so the president is from the family who has not had enough food [at times] and he or she has many struggles in their life. So that is the things that if people can, then why not people with disabilities? If women can, why not women with disabilities? That is the main things. Another is education is most important. If you do not have education, you could not open your eyes, you could not open your knowledge, you could not exercise the knowledge, and you could not get the dream in practical life, like this.

Misti's work has spanned from advocating for accessible buildings, through advocating for education, to helping other women and girls with disabilities see and use their power within. Misti's story highlights the importance of having support and networking with other women with disabilities in order to make progress towards change.

### Advocacy

I chose Misti's story to introduce the final theme of advocacy because of the lengths to which Misti had to go to get access to education through self-advocacy, and the widespread impact this has had: her own organization continues to work on advocacy efforts. Tika, Jane, and Amal have similar stories of experiencing discrimination and starting organizations to help others advocate for their rights.

By now, the challenges around advocacy should be clear. Other participants have described various advocacy strategies and efforts they have made through their work. Keegan advocates through social media sharing and participating in protests. Charlie and Patricia each describe advocating with women with mental health disabilities to ensure their rights and basic needs are met. Elizabeth describes working with her organization to help build women's capacity to advocate for their rights at home, in society, and in accessing support legally. Molly and Sarah have advocated at their universities and in their communities against gender-based violence in the disability community. Sarah has taken her advocacy efforts to the federal level.

What each of these participants has said is that their advocacy efforts have helped them feel a sense of community with the people they work with in eliminating gender-based violence. There is an element of empowerment that comes through in hearing these stories and, certainly, in the participants' desire to tell them.

As with the experiences identified in the previous chapter, identifying the transformations was the easier aspect of my analysis. The transformations were more difficult to describe in isolation. They easily overlap, and appear to work collectively to lead to transformation for the participants. All of the participants are educated, and many spoke about the importance of getting an education. One of the ways they wanted better for others was for others to also have access to education. It could be said of many of the participants that they want better for others because they see themselves in the work they do and in the other women and girls they work with. Others did not initially see themselves represented and they want others like them to not feel that way, too.

What keeps the participants hopeful is that there is more awareness among communities, and other people with disabilities, about gender-based violence and disability. Their methods to create better for others and raise awareness often take the form of advocacy work. Perhaps the strongest message, that comes from participants time and again, is that they get strength from working with others towards a collective goal. The work can be challenging, emotionally draining, and endless, but feeling a collective sense of purpose and shared goals seems to be a driving force.

## Notes

1. See The Legislative Assembly of Manitoba site for the full text of the Act at https://web2.gov.mb.ca/bills/41-1/b015e.php
2. #MeToo emerged in 2017 encouraging women to publicly share their experiences of sexual assault and harassment. See Kampen (2018).

# CHAPTER 6
# Conclusion

Chapter 2 provided a theoretical framework for understanding oppression. Intersectionality was introduced as an important element of this work because the historical exclusion of women with disabilities from multiple movements indicates a failure to understand intersectional oppression. This research supports previous findings that women and trans people with disabilities have been excluded from feminist and disability movements. This was mentioned by several participants whose work spans decades. While intersectionality was mentioned directly by some participants in terms of addressing various aspects of identity in this work, an intersectional analysis requires moving beyond recognizing multiple aspects of identity, a point to which I return shortly.

Working through the material conditions of oppression and contributions to disability oppression, laid the groundwork for looking at disability consciousness and empowerment. Charlton's work, described in the second chapter, is closely related to my project. Where his work departs from mine is that he does not address gender-based violence or intersectional analysis. My contribution here is to begin to fill the gap in research on the material conditions that set the stage for empowering people with disabilities who experience gender-based violence. This final chapter brings together my theoretical foundations and my findings to understand what oppression, consciousness, and empowerment look like in the day-to-day lives of organizers and advocates. The themes align with Charlton's work in that elements of participant experiences have been oppressive while the transformative themes outline conditions of empowerment, though, as discussed, the experiences and transformative themes overlap.

It is my hope that the elements of intersectionality that were introduced in the theory chapter can be seen throughout my findings. I want to deliberately employ an intersectional analysis in this final chapter. My objectives in doing so are threefold: 1) to highlight the complexity of the experiences and community organizing work identified by the participants in this study; 2) to further situate myself as the researcher and my relationship to this project; and 3) to offer a way forward and recommendations to further address gender-based violence in the disability community.

I reiterate Hankivsky's (2012) eight principles of an intersectional analysis because I will be using these as I work through my findings. They are: A) recognizing intersecting categories; B) multi-level analysis; C) power; D) reflexivity; E) understanding time and space; F) valuing diverse knowledges; G) social justice; and H) equity.

**Intersecting categories** reminds us that social categories are not mutually exclusive. They interact with and co-constitute one another, resulting in unique social locations.

**Multi-level analysis**, the second principle, looks at experiences across various levels of society ranging from individual through grassroots, community, regional, provincial, and national to global levels. It is the relationship between various structures and social locations that are important to this analysis.

**Power** operates at all levels to include and exclude knowledge and experiences. Our social locations and categories are informed by processes and systems of power and how these processes and systems interact to impact our experiences of privilege or oppression.

**Reflexivity**, the fourth principle, helps us to address the abovementioned power dynamics by acknowledging the ways it affects all areas of our lives. Reflexivity recognizes power within ourselves. It also recognizes our relationship to others. Being reflexive offers a transformative potential through critical self-awareness, questioning of power, and questioning what is believed to be true.

Intersectional analysis acknowledges that our experiences are not fixed. **Time and space**, the fifth principle, recognizes that our lived experiences are heavily influenced by our social position and location. This means that what we understand about the world, or how we interpret it, can change over time.

The sixth principle of **diverse knowledge** is important. Knowledge from the marginalized and excluded is especially important in order to address the power dynamics involved in producing knowledge. There is a diverse range of knowledge and experience to be generated from qualitative research like that in the present study.

The seventh principle is **social justice** and it is a driving force behind my desire (and that of others) to pursue this work. It is important for working towards equity and challenging the power relations that uphold inequality and discrimination.

Closely related to social justice is the final principle of **equity** which is concerned with fairness. It is the focus on difference, not sameness, that is important here. Whereas equality treats everyone the same, equity focuses on what is fair, taking into account that we have different social locations and experiences.

Using an intersectional analysis, I will work through the themes in order to address my argument that organizers emerge when they have supports in place, and that movements to end violence can transform consciousness about oppression. While I will attempt to identify how the various principles of intersectional analysis are used in my findings by naming them, it will become evident that, for many of these issues, several principles will be operating at the same time. The next sections look at the material conditions needed in the transformation from oppression to consciousness and, finally, to empowerment.

## Gender and disability oppression

As discussed throughout this book, many of us with disabilities did not grow up in a community of 'people like us.' Many of our families do not comprise people with disabilities, nor do we receive cultural cues from our families. If we are lucky, we have parents who advocate for us, or understand that we are equal and treat us equitably. If we are not lucky, we are hidden from society or abused, maybe out of desperation. The contradiction that the disability community faces, Charlton (1998) said, was that people with disabilities are isolated and stigmatized and, at the same time, they are expected to unite around common experiences of oppression while accommodating difference. What if that isolation and stigmatization is further complicated by gender?

Intersectional analysis is important here. As a theory, intersectionality gives us an understanding that we cannot separate parts of identity or understand them as additive. They work together to form our experiences and shape our experience of oppression. The historical absence of women and trans people with disabilities from the disability movement, and from anti-violence and gender movements, has been studied and highlighted in previous research. As noted, many of the people I interviewed acknowledge this historical absence and how it has consequences in the present day. Despite the continued oppression of women, girls, and trans people with disabilities, challenges remain in the movements. Invisibility within movements is itself oppressive. While some participants started their own organizations to represent women with disabilities and work against violence in its many forms, some also acknowledged that more work is being done to address gender-based violence in the disability community, and this keeps them hopeful.

In other words, oppression is intersectional, and the disability and feminist movements have historically had trouble seeing that they should be connected to each other. There was fear among people involved in the disability movement that addressing additional forms of oppression would take away from the energy or resources in the movement. The participants in this research who started organizations for women with disabilities did so because they recognized that their social categories interact and co-constitute one another (to draw on Hankivsky's first principle). They spoke about actively resisting men's efforts to lead their organizations. There seems to be a misguided belief by men in the movement that because some of the women had not previously led an organization, they did not know how to do it. In reality, women are just as capable as men but are often prevented from demonstrating this.

If we think about oppression as the denial of power, and we should, then power dynamics are critical. We have seen that, historically, one group within the disability movement (men with disabilities) has sought to control another (women with disabilities) through an institutional process of domination that long remained unquestioned. These groups are not opposed to one another, but there is a lack of support for gender inclusion in the disability movement.

It is also becoming increasingly clear that trans people with disabilities face similar challenges to having their experiences included in gender or disability movements. There is a long history of people with disabilities experiencing isolation and oppression perpetrated by those without disabilities, but there can be oppression within movements as well. Research on oppression has highlighted the ways in which those who are oppressed will then seek to oppress others in order to feel more powerful. Freire discusses the consciousness of the oppressed in a way that usefully unpacks the issues. He says:

> At a certain point in their existential experience the oppressed feel an irresistible attraction towards the oppressors and their way of life. Sharing this way of life becomes an overpowering aspiration. In their alienation, the oppressed want at any cost to resemble the oppressors, to imitate them, to follow them (1970: 62).

There are still tensions between those who dominate disability movements and those who do not. One person I interviewed describes her feelings about men with disabilities and their treatment of women with disabilities. She offers an explanation as to why some men with disabilities abuse women with disabilities:

> I have really conflicting feelings about disabled men right now. Where, I think disabled men have kind of an incel[1] mentality, of having been denied sex so many times because of sexual ableism that they then perpetrate violence on disabled women. And I think that is something that is still very challenging and gross in our community and hasn't changed at all. I think it's also a growing problem. But, beyond that, I mean, I think, it's the most marginalized within our groups that are having to do all this work and I think it's hard because so many of us are still struggling to be legally allowed into a building, you know? So, it's hard to have this other conversation too where right now we only have space for so many things because it's like, 'We can only have two issues.' But we have so many because we're neglected.

Perhaps, in this case, men with disabilities want to be like men without disabilities and, if this participant is correct, they want to have access to the same privileges they perceive as being available to non-disabled men. There is no way to delve into the psyche of men with disabilities who perpetrate violence against women with disabilities but, if theories of oppression are valid, then one possibility is that the dynamics Freire describes still exist in the disability community. Additionally, when there is competition, then the most marginalized remain invisible in the movement.

Our histories have been erased; or, even worse, they have not been considered long enough to have even been written in the first place. Disability inclusion has improved through the efforts of people with disabilities and our allies, but gender-based violence in the disability community still remains largely invisible and unacknowledged. When I told people about my research, men would often say to me, 'Violence against women with disabilities? Is that even a thing? Does that even happen?' Where does this question come from? I cannot say for sure if the underlying assumption is that women with disabilities are so helpless that no one would want to hurt us, or if it is that women with disabilities are so undesirable that no one would even want to spend enough time with us to hurt us. Whatever the assumption, it is that we are less valuable, less powerful. Further still, conversations about trans people with disabilities and violence did not surface at all when I discussed my research with those same folks.

Participants discussed the lack of understanding about intersectionality on the part of policy makers and decision-makers, and the implications that this has for women and trans people with disabilities and those working to support them. In material terms, we have seen that programmes and supports are designed to screen people out or exclude them. Those working to support other women have done the hard work of self-reflection on their role as part of these systems. This has not stopped them from acknowledging their part. Instead, they work to be more supportive. A multi-level analysis encourages us to understand experiences between and across various levels of society (Hankivsky, 2012).

Participants described experiencing a wide range of abuse and oppression from a young age into later adulthood. Some experienced negative perceptions in their communities about women with disabilities and their ability to have relationships; some experienced extensive barriers trying to access basic education; others experienced abuse at university, or harassment when trying to enter the workforce; and still others were institutionalized. These challenges have underlying conditions of powerlessness. Powerlessness is a predominant form of oppression (Freire 1970; Young, 1980). When people do not have decision-making powers, they are moved from subject to object. This dehumanization was discussed by some participants and given among the reasons they do the work to resist violence. This was seen in Molly's case:

> I was assaulted and then forcibly institutionalized because I came forward about my assault. It was a horrible experience and I think one that we don't recognize how much power institutions have. My university was the one who mandated it. How is that legal? And then, also, why are perceptions of people talking about sexual violence [such that we] still only label them as crazy?

The previous chapters also highlight some of the abuse and structural violence that contribute to or perpetuate oppression which participants have witnessed against other women and girls.

Intersectional oppression is also evident in the lack of policy and government commitment to eradicating violence against women and trans people with disabilities. Many of the participants specifically spoke about this lack of government commitment. In the face of inadequately resourced systems and services, funding that is given is often directed to other priorities, such as providing security in institutions rather than effective treatment or support for people with mental health concerns; and services that impact women and trans people with disabilities experiencing violence are cut, for example, libraries that might provide a safe haven, or payment tokens in the Toronto Transit System. How, then, will agencies in Toronto who might have previously have given tokens offer transit support?

Now imagine that you experience violence, and you work up the courage or find the resources to leave your situation and report your abuser, only to be met with further barriers. Barriers to accessing justice were described time and again by participants in my research. We have heard stories of young girls seeking recourse to justice for violence and abuse they have experienced only to be told that they are too poor to win their cases, or that they will still have to see their abuser every day after making a complaint.

Structural violence was a predominant theme that emerged in the interviews and stories: respite centres putting young women with disabilities at risk of sexual violence in Australia; physical and chemical restraint of people experiencing a mental health crisis in Canada. Violence goes beyond intimate partner violence. Violence can be experienced when a person feels forced to identify with a pathologizing diagnosis in order to get access or rights to a service or support. Or when programmes are not open to people with disabilities because of an unfounded fear that the institution will be subjected to additional risk of liability. In these cases, community advocates may then need to find ways to work around these restrictions in order to reach those most in need of services.

The examples given by the participants in the study offer unique insight into the everyday material conditions that are oppressive at the personal, professional, institutional, and government levels – but these people have worked towards change for themselves and others.

## Moving to consciousness about disability oppression

As described in the second chapter, Charlton noted that people with disabilities are susceptible to experiencing false consciousness about their disability in the form of helplessness, or lack of self-appreciation, or perhaps through feeling shame and self-hate. Though it is important, I want to speak only briefly about internalized oppression here. De Beauvoir (1949:2011) said that women have been Othered by men in order for men to maintain control over women. Girls are socialized from a young age to have feminine traits. Historical experiences, de Beauvoir said, alter a girl's perception of her reality.

What happens when women are unable to meet the standard of normalized feminine traits? What if her disability affects her ability to perform her gender in expected ways (Butler, 1990)? Or what if she is perceived as unable to perform her gender roles? Where do trans people with disabilities fit into this conversation? As already discussed, some of the participants spoke specifically about being unmarried or without a family because of perceptions about them as women with disabilities. Shakespeare (2006) confronts the reality that there may be negative effects of impairment such as pain or discomfort. But we are not encouraged to talk about this for fear of perpetuating negative perceptions or stereotypes about disability. This can lead to negative self-perceptions. It is important to note, though, that these negative perceptions and stereotypes are also influenced by gender norms that are shifting, but not fast enough. If you are a man with a disability, perhaps your pain is an affront to your masculinity. If you are a woman, pain and discomfort does not sit well with perceptions of beauty or grace, or even caregiving.

Goffman's (1963) and Hughes' (1999) work on stigma and the gaze is interesting here. When people experience oppression based on several aspects of identity, they might not even know for certain why the staring – the gaze – is upon them. The staring and the gaze create unease which is further complicated by the additional possibility of having violence enacted upon us based on our gender. When society continuously tells you that you do not fit into your gender role, while you are always under the gaze of those without disabilities, then enter the shame and self-hate that Charlton (1998) talked about. Trans people with disabilities, it has been found, live with the cumulative effects of transness and disability at the intersection of at least two marginalized identities (often more, considering other aspects of identity that cannot be isolated) and this is experienced as an additional difficulty (Baril et al., 2020).

Participants were open about their experiences of violence or isolation. They shared an understanding of their oppressive experiences being tied to their disability identity, often to their gender, and often to wider systemic issues. Many of the participants in this study, when asked why they do what they do, expressed anger about their experiences. When they discussed barriers, some talked about being denied access to education and then working to prove themselves capable. There was a sense that this was wrong, and one participant specifically pointed out that because of her efforts to succeed in university, other students with disabilities would also be granted access. Not only did the participant feel empowered, she was also able to help others in the process. This is an example of the resistance to oppression described by Hughes', requiring a refusal 'to be seen as one is supposed to be seen by the eye of power, to return the gaze and transform shame and humiliation into pride' (1999: 162). This participant was seen as being incapable of achieving a higher academic standing but refused to accept this false perception enacted upon her.

Charlton (1998) tells us that recognizing a common experience of oppression is critical for developing a raised consciousness. When participants work with other women with disabilities, they are at once recognizing a common experience and working to change it. In some cases, the participants described challenges to making other people with disabilities aware of their rights, but this is something they worked to do. A particular theme that emerged in the stories was one of community organizing. The participants spoke about the many ways they worked with other people to advance common interests.

The move to consciousness of disability and disability oppression was seen in participants' recognition that when they experienced violence, they were not personally responsible for what had happened to them. Rather they reached out to other women with disabilities and began to realize that those women shared similar experiences. At least one participant spoke about the difficulties in coming to terms with their own experience being reflected in their work. Much of this had to do with internalized ableism and a fear of contributing to the perception that women with disabilities are vulnerable. But the point then becomes that they do the work: they fight for resources, and for other women and trans people with disabilities experiencing abuse and violence. One participant indicated that she felt stronger because of her work with other women with disabilities.

Trans participants talked about doing the work they do because they did not see aspects of their identity, namely their experience of gender, reflected in the movements they were involved in. Experiences of gender, disability, and violence are complex for people whose gender identity places them outside the margins: their framing of disability does not fit with mainstream disability movements, and their experiences of violence are inextricably linked to both. Consider also how citizenship or socio-economic status, race, and age may also impact experiences of violence and reactions to it. The truth is, my research did not reach the depths I would have liked it to on issues related to gender identity, but I view my work as a starting point, not an end point.

Usha's stories of working with communities to get other girls with disabilities away from violence and into schools speaks to her consciousness of disability oppression. Though Usha initially faced barriers to education due to being blind, her family allowed her to go to school and gave her independence when she went to work. When she met young girls in communities who were kept at home in difficult environments, not given a chance to go out to school, she was compelled to act, often describing the difficult emotions that came with this. She recognized the importance of education in her own life and sought to ensure the same for others.

We know that, historically, there was not a disability community per se. As the disability rights movement began to emerge, so too did people who identified as having a disability. In this sense, a community has developed – albeit a diverse one. With the exception of the Deaf community, and perhaps a few others, people are generally not born into a disability community. One must therefore first identify as having a disability before a raised consciousness about it is available. It is important to not only work to change external perceptions of disability, but also internal ones.

Many women with disabilities internalize ableism, as we have discussed. Interestingly, only one participant spoke specifically about disability pride. Sarah, in the United States, did not speak about negative self-perceptions after acquiring her disability. She spoke about experiencing violence but she also spoke about disability being an important part of who she is. Specifically, she talks about pride and empowerment connected to her disability identity. To repeat her sentiments:

> I'm really involved in the disability pride movement. Because I'm someone who so, so, so strongly believes that disability is one of my favourite things about who I am and I'm so proud of it. And so I fight a lot for the cultural model of disability and moving forward with that aspect, focusing on identity and empowerment.

This does not mean that other participants did not feel pride. I would argue that many of the participants, in describing their work and efforts to end violence, certainly showed pride in their accomplishments. Several participants, when asked to describe their work, had no trouble identifying a long list of important contributions they have made in their communities. That this information was so easily available to them demonstrates to me a sense of awareness about the impact of their work and the importance of it to them. We must also remember that these participants have worked within a movement that has historically favoured men and ignored the serious issue of violence against women and trans-people with disabilities.

Let us talk about freedom. Critical race theorists have told us that people do not act or resist because they fear freedom. They tell us that turning silence into language is an act of self-revelation and this can be dangerous for those who do not have the resources to be safe in the face of danger if they do speak their truth. But these patterns need to be exposed in order to move toward change.

My research leads me to agree with Freire that education is critical for raising consciousness and self-awareness, but the fear of freedom in speaking truth is a reality for many women with disabilities, especially when they are institutionalized or further traumatized when they do speak the truth. Some do so anyway. Many participants described advocating for their own rights, and with other women with disabilities for their rights across time and space, whether it was with families, at institutions, or with governments. The participants in the study who experienced oppression, being aware that it was not their fault, reached out to other women to organize and advocate. They had the resources to do so, whether it was family support or access to education. Through this process they are able to support others as well as change their perceptions of their own experiences. We turn now to empowerment as the final phase of the process that community organizers move through.

## Empowerment of advocates working against gender-based violence

If Duncan (1999) is right that personal experiences contribute to group consciousness and that group consciousness then leads to collective action, then the participants in this study who speak of working with communities or of starting their own organizations have moved through one such process. To move from a raised consciousness to an empowered consciousness, Charlton (1998) explained, is to commit to act upon one's raised consciousness. Importantly, as argued by Freire:

> The oppressed must confront reality critically, simultaneously objectifying and acting upon that reality. A mere perception of reality not followed by this critical intervention will not lead to a transformation of objective reality – precisely because it is not a true perception. (1970: 52)

Elements of an empowered consciousness showed up in my research in several ways. When I asked participants why they do what they do or what keeps them going, they told me about the various ways they networked with other people experiencing gender-based violence in the disability community. They describe specific actions they had taken to move forward: in some cases, it was to find women who shared common experiences in order to build an organization of women with disabilities to combat violence and oppression; in other cases, people in the community called upon them to help with abuse cases and they answered by reaching out to their networks to help. They spoke about the momentum that was gained through working with other women with disabilities. Some participants did advocacy work on campuses, others worked with communities, some met with politicians, others lost their jobs when they spoke out about abuse.

Of course, there are still divisions in the disability community. One such disconnect was between those advocating for women with physical disabilities and those for women with psychiatric or mental health disabilities. If it was discussed by participants, it was primarily discussed by those who identified as experiencing both. For example, one participant said:

> I really try to work a lot on, like, cross-disability organizing because I think our community is really divided. Especially, I have both a physical and a psychiatric disability so I really have tried to bring the community together and make sure that we're not putting each other down to bring ourselves up.

Even when there are limitations the inclination is to bridge the gaps in order to strengthen solidarity.

A prominent theme was wanting a better situation for other women and trans people with disabilities. This was often expressed after the participants spoke about seeing aspects of their identity and experience in the work, or not. As already discussed, many participants expressed a desire to create a better environment to support women with disabilities experiencing abuse and oppression. It was a motivator and a driver for many of the participants. The feeling expressed in the question 'How can I not do something?' to me is a manifestation of empowered consciousness. It means that women and trans people with disabilities have experienced oppression but then feel compelled to help others avoid similar situations.

Raised awareness was a final motivator for the participants in my research. They speak about wanting a better situation for others, but they also express satisfaction that society is becoming more aware of the issues affecting women with disabilities. There are more people fighting against a wider range of issues. This was seen as progress by some. In some cases, participants told me that the women they work with are more aware of their rights because of their efforts. In other cases, women with disabilities were taking on more leadership roles and had more support available to them, and this motivated participants to continue supporting other women with disabilities. The themes that emerged in this study align with Charlton's (1998) theorization of the conditions necessary for change. He talked about moving between oppression, false consciousness, raised consciousness, and empowered consciousness. The experiences shared by the people I interviewed give insight into the material conditions that coincide with this process.

Barnartt's (1996) three processes involved in resisting oppression are also relevant. The first is consensus formation: personal troubles are viewed as shared rather than an individual problem. People with disabilities now see themselves as an oppressed group. It is also necessary, though, for women and trans people with disabilities to see their additional experiences of oppression as also based on their gender. Diverse knowledge from women and trans people with disabilities who are marginalized in society and in both disability and women's movements is needed in order to fully understand and address power dynamics. Participants with disabilities who started organizations started by talking to other people. It was only through connecting that they were able to move beyond their individual experiences.

The second process is consensus mobilization. This can be seen in the way the participants found solidarity in sharing common experiences of violence.

The third and final process is action mobilization which we see when organizations form and people collaborate towards ending gender-based violence in the disability community. So, while this analysis is correct and critical to our understanding of disability oppression, consciousness, and empowerment, Barnartt's work does not address intersectionality or offer an intersectional analysis.

## The path to empowerment is not linear, cyclical or parallel

I pursued this research because I wanted to understand more directly how experiences of oppression relate to the move to consciousness and the ultimate goal of empowerment. I wanted to understand the connection between these processes when we talk about gender-based violence in the disability community because this remains a reality for so many.

Internalized oppression is important to me. There is a psychological component that keeps drawing me back in while I also give attention to structures, to the environment, and to society. It is because of my own experiences and what I have come to understand about myself, in large part due to writing my Ph.D dissertation. As a woman with a disability, for a long time I did not understand that my experiences with violence are part of a larger problem rooted in a long history of oppression. It is only through learning this that I felt a compulsion to do something about it.

I began my dissertation research believing that the process of moving from oppression, to consciousness, to empowerment is linear, or maybe cyclical. It is not necessarily so. It can be cyclical to some extent, or perhaps parallel, and it is not always progressive. We still experience oppression after becoming conscious of it. We can experience oppression after we become empowered to fight against it. The participant stories were not linear. Many of them talked about doing the work, but also experiencing discrimination or violence at the same time. This is part of the reason why I chose to tell all of the participant stories in their complete form, because their stories could not be fully understood by their parts alone. What was found in the stories was persistence. This persistence coupled with consciousness means that the process is not linear – but neither is it cyclical because the process changes once awareness and resistance are established.

Charlton (1998) said as long as oppression exists so too will people struggle against it. That is true, but it also means that as long as people with disabilities need to work to end gender-based violence because they feel empowered to do so, they will be met with oppression. They may continue to experience violence, so the resistance must also always be against oppression (both external and internal) at the same time. But, once you know you are oppressed, you cannot unknow it. Disability consciousness, then, cannot be undone. Charlton understood the complexities of consciousness:

> Consciousness, however, is not a linear progression. At points this quantitative buildup congeals into a 'rupture', or a qualitative or trans-formational leap to another stage of consciousness where another spiral-like phenomenon begins. Consciousness can leap from being-in-itself (existence as is) to being-for-itself (consciously desiring change) (1998: 28–29).

Empowerment is something we must constantly struggle to maintain. Once we have power, we must always work to keep it. Empowerment does not make us immune to oppression, but it does give us tools to resist it. In this sense, the process is not linear because at the same time that we are empowered we are still experiencing oppression.

Many of the participants in my study say they continue to do this work because of a feeling of 'How could I not act?' This compulsion to act does not relieve us of the burden of feeling bad about ourselves. We can still internalize the negative experiences we are working against. Once you have experienced consciousness and empowerment, perhaps then resistance becomes key. If you reach empowerment and experience oppression, your resistance to it is stronger because you have already established the conditions needed to reach empowerment (community support, education, and consciousness).

The process is not cyclical because the starting point to resist oppression after you reach empowerment is now different, perhaps elevated. Three possible process representations are shown in Figures 6.1–6.3.

In part, my argument proposes that movements to end violence can transform individual and collective consciousness about disability and gender oppression. What I did not consider, though, is that as long as organizers and the movements they belong to are needed, they will always be working through issues of oppression, consciousness, and empowerment at the same time. The end goal is not only empowerment, but to develop the capacity to maintain it.

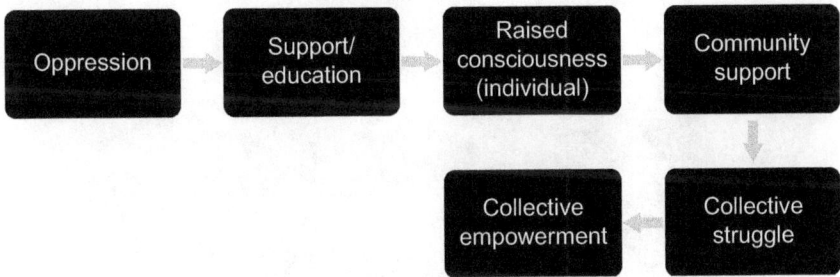

**Figure 6.1** Individual level moving into collective action

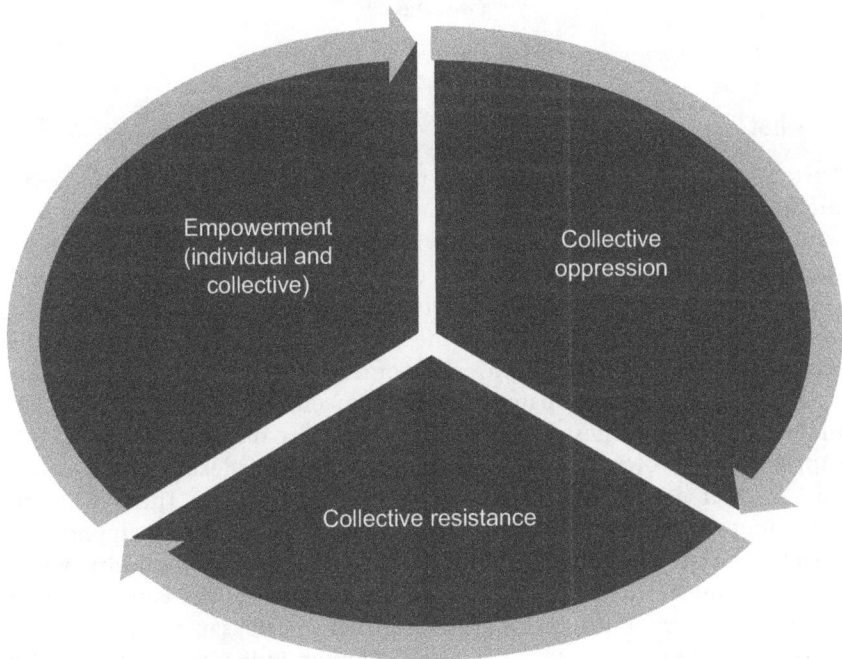

**Figure 6.2** After collective empowerment

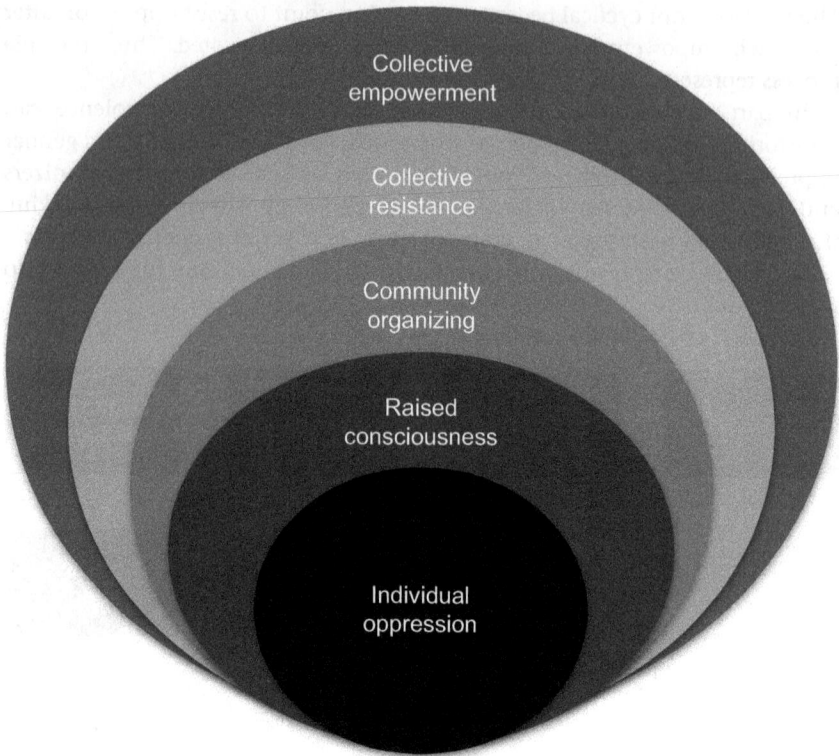

**Figure 6.3** Empowerment within social movements

## So what?

There appear to be two aspects to social movement organizing. The first aspect – the individual aspect – is where an individual experiences oppression but, with support and education, the individual experiences consciousness about their oppression based on gender and disability. With this consciousness and support, they are able to resist oppressive circumstances. It is with this feeling of resistance and consciousness that the individual may also participate in the second aspect which is social movement organizing.

A person may participate in social movement organizing with an individual consciousness and resistance that they have gathered through support in their own lives or through education. This leads them to reach out to other people who may have similar experiences. This I will call community support. It is with this networking and community support that people become empowered, both individually and as a community, while also engaging in collective resistance. So, then, personal empowerment and collective empowerment can be happening at the same time.

There is a second part to my analysis. Once an individual or community feels empowerment, this does not mean that their oppression ends. What we have now is a community experiencing oppression but with a collective understanding of their circumstances as oppressive, and an awareness of the possibility of taking action. Consciousness-raising may happen at the individual level and community level through social movements and, when they later experience oppression, they will already be empowered or have a different level of resistance to it. People and movements, then, can be experiencing oppression, resistance, and empowerment simultaneously. As Charlton (1998) says, they will have an empowered consciousness. But it will also be a new consciousness.

What does this mean for social movement organizing? I would argue that social movements are comprised of individuals who have consciousness of and resistance to their oppression which led them to seek community support in the first place. In order for social movements to be ongoing and progressive, they require supporters and actors who individually and as a collective recognize common oppressive experiences and share a desire to ensure better for themselves and others. This desire may come first through their individual consciousness and then from the empowerment they feel through their community organizing, which builds resistance for themselves and for the movement.

This is important for women and trans people with disabilities, who for so long have experienced gender-based violence but were met with resistance from any movement that would have helped them, had they had only the one identity marker the movement was focusing on. Newer advocates whom I interviewed are already expressing an understanding of identity as complicated, and that this needs to be further addressed in gender-based violence and disability movements. Perhaps it is because historically so many women and trans people with disabilities have had extensive experience being excluded that it becomes almost second nature to account for everyone in the room.

## Next steps

As we move forward, we must not be exclusionary. Given that participants identified a lack of policy and government support and commitment as a challenge; and given that evidence of empowerment for the participants in my study has been demonstrated through their wanting a better situation for others, and through networking with those who share similar experiences and priorities, a positive way forward is to approach government and policy makers to prioritize work on gender-based violence in the disability community. One strategy could be to develop a support network at the national or local level that could act as a central support place to connect women and trans people working on these issues. When people with disabilities mobilize to end gender-based violence, we know this can lead to them to establishing their own organizations. Connecting these organizations might further mobilize women and trans people with disabilities globally.

Current policies that address gender-based violence, employment and income support, rights and justice, need to be reviewed using the eight principles of Hankivsky's *Intersectionality Based Policy Analysis*. This should be approached with a view towards social justice and equity in the disability community, so that people with disabilities are supported in all areas of life and are empowered to live on an equitable basis with others.

Finally, the struggle to work against oppression is never done. Oppression is the original starting point. Consciousness follows when women and trans people with disabilities have access to education and/or support. This consciousness is necessary before advocates can work towards change. Education on all levels needs to be improved such that inclusion becomes the norm in classrooms, colleges, and universities. But also, social issues within educational settings need to address the historical and current structural issues of oppression. Efforts to accurately and more realistically present women and trans people with disabilities in media, news, and other public avenues would be a welcome start to preventing a false consciousness about what it means to be a woman, girl, or trans person with a disability. If people with disabilities were simply in movies or TV shows as common everyday people: being parents, spouses, employers, workers, athletes, leaders etc., then perhaps young people with disabilities would grow up believing they have a right to all of these things regardless of their identity.

Working towards change can be a signifier of empowerment, but it can also be a supporting element. Once empowerment is reached, and people with disabilities feel a sense of purpose in working to change their oppressive circumstances and those of other women, girls, and trans people with disabilities, the work is not done. Oppression may still occur. This is not a choice. What this does mean, though, is that when oppression occurs, we are now equipped to resist it more quickly. If this is true, then continuous community support within the movement is critical to its progress.

## Further questions

As I worked through analysis of the interviews, questions arose about the relationship between mental health status and violence. One participant discussed violence as disabling and leading to mental health issues. This was not my initial approach to my study. My framing was to look at the gender-based violence experienced in the disability community and what led participants to advocate for change within the systems and structures that impeded recovery from their abuse, or which contributed to their abuse. The disability community comprises multiple forms of disability, multiple categories and experiences. I did not seek to analyse violence as disabling, though it can be. Further research could look more deeply into mental health, addiction, and experiences of violence.

A second area of research that was beyond the scope of the present study, but was addressed briefly, is violence towards and between support workers in the disability community, or towards support workers from the disability community – particularly aggression towards female support workers – and the consequences for support workers who attempt to expose abuse within support systems. This is an understudied and important area of research that requires further attention.

Finally, though my study included women and trans people, the experiences related specifically to trans identity did not surface to the extent I would have liked. There remains a significant opportunity to address violence based on trans identity and disability, and to include LGBTQI2S communities more intentionally in gender and disability-based violence work.

## Final reflections

Seeing my experience, to some extent, reflected in the theorizing of others has led me to recognize that my experiences are more than an anomaly and cannot be explained without considering my disability and gender identities. This recognition has forced me to confront the reality that I am a member of an oppressed group: a group that, by all accounts, has not historically been united by a single trait or experience or even by common experiences of oppression.

The disability movement has been fractured due to a hierarchy of disability and a fear that incorporating other aspects of identity would somehow weaken the movement to gain independence and rights for people with disabilities. We have seen that when people with disabilities were discussed historically, white, physically disabled, middle-class, heteronormative men have been disproportionately represented. The movement has historically catered to this section of the disability population and has represented oppressive experiences and discrimination in an often-singular way with a focus on accessibility. This has changed over time, of course, but these experiences are more complex and sometimes altogether different when additional elements of identity – gender, race, class, citizenship status, age, for example – are considered.

In terms of reflexivity, undertaking this project was at first empowering: seeing my experiences as a woman with a disability who has moved in and out of poverty throughout my life reflected, to some extent, in the stories told by the participants in my study. At the same time, though, as I have been writing and theorizing about my findings, it has become emotionally difficult work. At times, the stories have been difficult to work with. Also, my own self-perception has been in flux: some days I have felt as though I am less valuable because my body does not move like others; that this must be true because I have been subjected to violence and the person subjecting me to it must have considered me less valuable to be able to carry out violent acts upon me. Other days I feel empowered knowing that I am part of a larger group of people who have been unjustly characterized in the minds of strangers, and sometimes peers, and we are working toward change.

If I am to be completely honest, there were times when I have thought that, if society has reflected to me time and time again that to be a woman with a disability means that I am not capable, then maybe it is true. It has taken me longer than I wanted to complete my research because there have been full weeks where I have felt tired all the time. I have been excited about the idea of writing but unable to do it because I did not have the intellectual or emotional courage to accept my own findings. In the end, though, I have felt a transformation in how I see myself, driven primarily by how I have viewed the participants in my study and the people whose stories they have told. I feel a sense of purpose in exposing the hardships and the successes of addressing gender-based violence in the disability community because I see each and every person affected by these issues as valuable and equal. I have now extended this view to myself and for that I am grateful.

## Note

1.  Incel refers to involuntarily celibate men and is commonly used to refer to lonely men who are angry that they are unable to secure relationships with women and so they turn to the dark corners of the internet.

# References

Abberley, P. (1987) 'The concept of oppression and the development of a social theory of disability', *Disability, Handicap & Society* 2(1), 5–19 <https://doi.org/10.1080/02674648766780021> [accessed 10 March 2022].

ADD International. (2017) *Your Impact Report; Women and Girls' Edition*. ADD International. <https://www.add.org.uk/sites/default/files/2017_ImpactReport_Spring.pdf> [accessed 10 March 2022].

Arat-Koc, S. (2006) 'Whose social reproduction? Transnational motherhood and challenges to feminist political economy', in K. Bezanson & M. Luxton (Eds.), *Social reproduction: Feminist political economy challenges neo-liberalism*, pp. 75–92, McGill-Queen's University Press.

Asch, A. (2001). Critical Race Theory, Feminism, and Disability: Reflections on Social Justice and Personal identity. *Ohio State Law Journal, 62(1)*, 391–423.

Bannerji, H. (1995) *Thinking through: Essays on Feminism, Marxism and Anti-racism*. Women's Press.

Baril, A. (2015). Needing to Acquire a Physical Impairment/Disability: (Re) Thinking the Connections between Trans and Disability Studies through Transability. *Hypatia, 30*(1), 30–48. https://doi.org/10.1111/hypa.12113

Baril, A., Pullen Sansfaçon A. and Gelly, M. A. (2020). Digging beneath the Surface: When Disability Meets Gender Identity. *Canadian Journal of Disability Studies* 9(4), 1–23. <https://doi.org/10.15353/cjds.v9i4.666> [accessed 10 March 2022].

Barnartt, S. (1996) 'Disability culture or disability consciousness?', *Journal of Disability Policy Studies* 7(2), 1–19. <https://doi.org/10.1177/104420739600700201>

Barnes, C. (2003) 'What a difference a decade makes: Reflections on doing "emancipatory" disability research', *Disability & Society* 18(1), 3–17.

Barnes, C. (1996) 'Disability and the myth of the independent researcher', *Disability and Society* 11(1), 107–110.

Barnes, C. (1992) *Disabling Imagery and the Media: An Exploration of the Principles for Media Representations of Disabled People*. The British Council of Organizations of Disabled People & Ryburn Publishing Limited; Krumlin, Halifax.

Barnes, C. & Mercer, G. (2010) *Exploring Disability* (2nd ed.). Polity Press.

Bê, A. (2019) 'Feminism and disability: a cartography of multiplicity', in N. Watson, & A. Roulstone, (eds) *Routledge handbook of disability studies*, pp. 363–375. Routledge.

de Beauvoir, S. (1949: 2011) *The Second Sex* (1st Vintage Books ed.). (C. Borde, S. Malovany-Chevallier, & J. Thurman, tr.). Vintage Books. (Original work published 1949).

Beisland, L. A. and Mersland, R. (2014) 'Income characteristics and the use of microfinance services: Evidence from economically active persons with disabilities', *Disability & Society* 29(3), 417–430. <https://doi.org/10.1080/0 9687599.2013.816625> [accessed 10 March 2022].

Bernard, H. R. (2013). *Social Research Methods: Qualitative and Quantitative Approaches* (2nd ed.). SAGE Publications Ltd.

Bloom, S.S. (2008). *Violence Against Women and Girls: a Compendium of Monitoring and Evaluation Indicators*. USAID East Africa Regional Mission with the Inter-agency Gender Working Group (USAID), MEASURE Evaluation. <http://www.endvawnow.org/uploads/browser/files/M&E%20 Indicators-MEASURE-2008.pdf> [accessed 10 March 2022].

Braathen, S. H. and Kvam, M. H. (2008) 'Can anything good come out of this mouth?' Female experiences of disability in Malawi, *Disability & Society* 23(5), 461–474. <http://dx.doi.org/10.1080/09687590802177023> [accessed 10 March 2022].

Brownridge, D.A. (2006) 'Partner violence against women with disabilities: Prevalence, risk and explanations', *Violence Against Women* 12(9), 805–822. <http://dx.doi.org/10.1177/1077801206292681> [accessed 10 March 2022].

Bucik, A, Ptolemy, A, and A. Simpson. (2017). *Canada: Discrimination and Violence* against LGBTQI2S Persons with Disabilities. Egale Canada Human Rights Trust.

Buettgen, A. (2018). *From the Standpoint of People with Disabilities: An Institutional Analysis of Work in the Non-profit Sector.* Unpublished doctoral dissertation. Toronto ON: York University, School of Health Policy and Management. York Space Institutional Repository. <https://yorkspace.library.yorku.ca/ xmlui/handle/10315/34561> [accessed 10 March 2022].

Butler, J. (1990). *Gender Trouble: Feminism and the Subversion of Identity.* Routledge.

Canadian Broadcasting Corporation. (2020). *People with Disabilities Left out of the Conversation about Coping with COVID, Advocates say.* White Coat Black Art. <https://www.cbc.ca/radio/whitecoat/people-with-disabilities-left-out-of-the-conversation-about-coping-with-covid-advocates-say-1.5596863> [accessed 10 March 2022].

Canadian Women's Foundation. (2014). *Fact Sheet: Moving Women out of Violence.* <http://www.canadianwomen.org/facts-about-violence> [accessed 10 March 2022].

Carbado, D., Crenshaw, K., Mays, V. and Tomlinson, B. (2013) 'Intersectionality: Mapping the movements of a theory', *Du Bois Review: Social Science Research on Race* 10(2), 303–312. <https://doi.org/10.1017/S1742058X13000349> [accessed 10 March 2022].

Charlton, J. I. (1998) *Nothing About us Without us: Disability Oppression and Empowerment.* University of California Press.

Christodoulidis, E. (2019) 'Critical theory and the law: reflections on origins, trajectories and conjunctures', in E. Christodoulidis, R. Dukes, M. & Goldoni. (eds.), *Research handbook on critical legal theory*, pp. 2–26, Edward Elgar Publishing. <https://doi.org/10.4337/9781786438898> [accessed 10 March 2022].

Clark, N. (2012). Beyond the reflective practitioner. In J. Drolet, N. Clark, & H. Allen (Eds.), *Shifting Sites of Practice: Field Education in Canada* (pp. 79–95). Toronto: Pearson Education Canada, Inc.

Cohen, M.M., Forte, T., Du Mont, J., Hyman, I. and Romans, S. (2005) 'Intimate partner violence among Canadian women with activity limitations', *Journal of Epidemiology & Community Health* 59(10), 834–839. <http://dx.doi.org/10.1136/jech.2004.022467> [accessed 10 March 2022].

Collins, P. H. (2000) *Black Feminist Thought: Knowledge, Consciousness, and the Politics of Empowerment* (rev. 10th anniversary edn). Routledge.

Cramer, E., Gilson, S. and Depoy, E. (2004) 'Women with disability and experiences of abuse', *Journal of Human Behavior in the Social Environment* 7(3), 183–199.

Crawford, C. (2013) *Looking into Poverty: Income Sources of Poor People with Disabilities in Canada*. Institute for Research and Development on Inclusion and Society (IRIS) & Council of Canadians with Disabilities.

Crenshaw, K. (1989) 'Demarginalizing the intersection of race and sex: Black feminist critique of antidiscrimination doctrine, feminist theory and antiracist politics,' *University of Chicago Legal Forum* 1989, 139–168.

Czaja, R. & Blair, J. (2005) 'Selecting the method of data collection,' in *Designing surveys* (pp. 33–58). SAGE Publications Ltd.

Davis, A. Y. 1. (1983). *Women, Race & Class* (1st Vintage Books edn). Vintage Books.

Dawn, R. (2014) 'The politics of cinematic representation of disability: "the psychiatric gaze"' *Disability & Rehabilitation: an International. Multidisciplinary Journal* 36(6). 515–520.

Deming, M. E. (2018) 'Michelle E. Deming: Commentary on gender-based violence and trauma in marginalized populations of women: Role of biological embedding and toxic stress,' *Health Care for Women International* 39(10), 1158–1159. <https://www.tandfonline.com/doi/abs/10.1080/07399332.2018.1533353>.

DisAbled Women's Network of Canada (DAWN) (2019) *More than a Footnote: A Research* Report on Women and Girls with Disabilities in Canada. DAWN Canada.

DAWN (2013) *Women with Disabilities and Violence: Factsheet*. <https://www.dawncanada.net/issues/women-with-disabilities-and-violence/>.

Duncan, L. (1999) 'Motivation for collective action: group consciousness as mediator of personality, life experiences, and women's rights activism' *Political Psychology* 20(3), 611–635. <http://www.jstor.org/stable/3792164> [accessed 10 March 2022].

Durst, D., South, S. and Bluechardt, M. (2006) 'Urban First Nations people with disabilities speak out' *Journal of Aboriginal Health* 3(1), 34–43.

Eisenstein, Z. (1999) 'Constructing a theory of capitalist patriarchy and socialist feminism' *Critical Sociology (Brill Academic Publishers)* 25(2/3), 196–217.

Erevelles, N. & Minear, A. (2013) 'Unspeakable offences: untangling race and disability discourses of intersectionality' in L. Davis (ed.), *The Disability studies reader* (pp. 354–368). Routledge.

Erevelles, N. (2011). *Disability and Difference in Global Contexts: Enabling a Transformative Body Politic*. Palgrave Macmillan.

European Institute for Gender Equality. (2016) *What is Gender Based Violence?* <http://eige.europa.eu/gender-based-violence/what-is-gender-based-violence> [accessed 10 March 2022].

Falcón, S. M. and Nash, J. C. (2015) 'Shifting analytics and linking theories: A conversation about the "meaning-making" of intersectionality and transnational feminism', *Women's Studies International Forum, 50*, 1–10.

Ferree, M. M. (2009). Inequality, intersectionality and the politics of discourse: Framing feminist alliances. In E. Lombardo, P. Meier, and M. Verloo (Eds.), *The discursive politics of gender equality: Stretching, bending and policy-making* (pp. 86–104). London: Routledge.

Finkelstein, V. (2001). *A Personal Journey into Disability Politics.* First presented at Leeds University Centre for Disability Studies, 2001. <http://www.independentliving.org/docs3/finkelstein01a.pdf> [accessed 10 March 2022].

Flanders, N. (2020) *Horrific: Texas man with Disability Dies after Doctors Refuse to Treat him for COVID-19.* Live Action. <https://www.liveaction.org/news/texas-disability-dies-doctors-refuse-covid-19/> [accessed 10 March 2022].

Foucault, M. (1977). *Discipline and punish.* London: Allen Lane.,

Freire, P. (1970) *Pedagogy of the Oppressed.* Herder and Herder.

Galvin, R. D. (2005) 'Researching the disabled identity: Contextualising the identity transformations which accompany the onset of impairment,' *Sociology of Health & Illness* 27(3), 393–413. <https://doi.org/10.1111/j.1467-9566.2005.00448.x> [accessed 10 March 2022].

Garland-Thomson, R. (2011), Misfits: A Feminist Materialist Disability Concept. *Hypatia* 26, 591–609. <https://doi.org/10.1111/j.1527-2001.2011.01206.x> [accessed 27 March 2022].

Garland-Thomson, R. (2006) 'Ways of Staring', *Journal of Visual Culture* 5(2), 173–192. <https://doi.org/10.1177/1470412906066907> [accessed 10 March 2022].

Ghai, A. (2002) 'Disabled women: an excluded agenda of Indian feminism,' *Hypatia* 17(3), 49–66. <https://doi.org/10.1111/j.1527-2001.2002.tb00941.x> [accessed 10 March 2022].

Gill, A. and Rehman, G. (2004) 'Empowerment through activism: Responding to domestic violence in the south Asian community in London,' *Gender & Development, 12*(1), 75–82.

Global Action on Disability Network. (2020). *General Statement of the GLAD Inclusive Education Working Group in Response to the COVID-19 Crisis.* <https://gladnetwork.net/search/resources/general-statement-glad-inclusive-education-working-group-response-covid-19-crisis> [accessed 10 March 2022].

Goethals, T., De Schauwer, E. and Van Hove, G. (2015) 'Weaving intersectionality into disability studies research: inclusion, reflexivity and anti-essentialism,' *DiGeSt. Journal of Diversity and Gender Studies* 2(1–2), 75–94. <https://www.jstor.org/stable/10.11116/jdivegendstud.2.1-2.0075#metadata_info_tab_contents>.

Goffman, E. (1963) *Stigma Notes on the Management of Spoiled Identity.* Aronson.

Goffman, E. (1962) *Asylums: Essays on the Social Situation of Mental Patients and other Inmates.* Aldine Pub. Co. <http://www.esdc.gc.ca/en/reports/rpp/2016_2017/index.page> [accessed 10 March 2022].

Gorman, R. (2007) 'The feminist standpoint and the trouble with 'informal learning': A way forward for Marxist-feminist educational research,' in

T. Green, G. Rikowski & H. Raduntz (eds), *Renewing dialogues in Marxism and education: Openings* (pp. 183–189). Palgrave Macmillan.

Haller, B. & Ralph, S. (2002) 'Profitability, diversity, and disability images in advertising in the United States and Great Britain,' *Disability Studies Quarterly* 21(2).

Hanifie, S. (2020) *Auslan Service Deaf NT Closes as Clients Struggle Through Coronavirus*. ABC News. <https://www.abc.net.au/news/2020-06-30/deaf-nt-auslan-service-closes-in-darwin-coronavirus/12403406> [accessed 10 March 2022].

Hankivsky, O. (ed.). (2012) *An Intersectionality-based Policy Analysis Framework*. Vancouver, BC: Institute for Intersectionality Research and Policy, Simon Fraser University. <https://data2.unhcr.org/en/documents/download/46176> [accessed 10 March 2022].

Hoefmans, A. & de Beco, G. (2010) *The UN Convention on the Rights of Persons with Disabilities: an Integral and Integrated Approach to the Implementation of Disability Rights*. Belgium, Federal Public Service.

hooks, b. (1996) *Reel to Real: Race, Sex, and Class at the Movies*. Routledge.

Hosking, D.L. (2008, September 2–4) *Critical Disability Theory* (Paper presentation). 4th Biennial Disability Studies Conference at Lancaster University, UK. <https://www.lancaster.ac.uk/fass/events/disabilityconference_archive/2008/papers/hosking2008.pdf> [accessed 10 March 2022].

Hughes, B. (1999) 'The constitution of impairment: modernity and the aesthetic of oppression,' *Disability & Society* 14(2), 155–172. <https://doi.org/10.1080/09687599926244> [accessed 10 March 2022].

International Labor Organization (ILO). (2015) *Inclusion of People with Disabilities in National Employment Policies*. <http://www.ilo.org/global/topics/disability-and-work/WCMS_407646/lang--en/index.htm> [accessed 10 March 2022].

International Network of Women with Disabilities (INWWD). (2010) *Document on Violence Against Women with Disabilities*.

Israel, P. & Odette, F. (1993) 'The disabled women's movement 1983 to 1993,' *Canadian Woman Studies* 13(4), 6–8.

Janghorban, R., Roudsari, R. L. and Taghipour, A. (2014) 'Skype interviewing: The new generation of online synchronous interview in qualitative research,' *International Journal of Qualitative Studies on Health and Well-being* 9(1), 1–3.Kafer. (2013). *Feminist, queer, crip*. Indiana University Press.

Kampen, M. (2018) *The facts: The #MeToo Movement and its Impact in Canada*. Canadian Women's Foundation. <https://canadianwomen.org/the-facts/the-metoo-movement-in-canada/> [accessed 10 March 2022].

Kanter, A. S. (2011) Law: What's Disability Studies got to do with it or an Introduction to Disability Legal Studies. *Columbia Human Rights Law Review, 42*, 403–480.

Kayess, R. (2011) *CRPD: International Cooperation and Development*. (Presentation handout). Summer School on the Convention on the Rights of Persons with Disabilities.

Kelm, M.E. (1992) '"The only place likely to do her any good": the admission of women to British Columbia's Provincial Hospital for the Insane (1905–1915),' *BC Studies, 96*, 66–89.

Kendall, K. (1999) Beyond grace: criminal lunatic women in Victorian Canada. *Canadian Woman Studies, 19* (1/2), 110–115.

Kennedy, E. L. (2008) 'Socialist Feminism: What Difference Did It Make to the History of Women's Studies?' *Feminist Studies* 34(3), 497–525.

Klandermans, B. (1984). Mobilization and participation: Social-psychological expansion of resource mobilization theory. *American Sociological Review,* 49, 583-600.

Klandermans, B. (1988). The formation and mobilization of consensus. In B. Klandermans, H. Kriesi, & S. Tarrow (Eds.), *International social movement research, vol. 1* (pp. 173–196). Greenwich, CT: JAI Press.

Klandermans, B. (1991). New social movements and resource mobilization: The European and the American approach revisited. In D. Rucht (Ed.), *Research on social movements: The state of the art in Western Europe and the USA* (pp. 17–44). Boulder, CO: Westview Press.

Klandermans, B. (1992). The social construction of protest and multi-organizational fields. In A. D. Morris & C. M. Mueller (Eds.), Frontiers in social movement theory (pp. 77–103). New Haven, CT: Yale University Press.

Krell, E. (2017). Is Transmisogyny Killing Trans Women of Color? Black Trans Feminisms and the Exigencies of White Femininity. *Transgender Studies Quarterly*, 4(2), 226–242.

Lalonde, D., Abramovich, A., Baker, L. and Tabibi, J. (2018) *LGBTQI2S Youth, Violence, and Homelessness.* Learning Network Newsletter, Issue 24. London, Ontario: Centre for Research & Education on Violence Against Women & Children. ISBN 978-1-988412-18-4

Lindqvist, B. (2015) 'Background: Monitoring – a key element in realizing human rights for all,' in M. H. Rioux, P. C. Pinto, & G. Parekh (eds). *Disability, rights monitoring, and social change: Building power out of evidence.* (pp. 13–24). Canadian Scholars' Press.

Lo Iacono, V., Symonds, P. and Brown, D.H.K. (2016) 'Skype as a tool for qualitative research interviews,' *Sociological Research Online* 21(2). <http://www.socresonline.org.uk/21/2/12.html> [accessed 10 March 2022].

Loja, E., Costaa, M.E., Hughes B, & Menezes, I. (2013) 'Disability, embodiment and ableism: stories of resistance,' *Disability & Society 28*(2), 190–203. <http://dx.doi.org/10.1080/09687599.2012.705057> [accessed 10 March 2022].

Lorde, A. (1984) *Sister Outsider: Essays and Speeches.* Trumansburg, NY: The Crossing Press.

Malacrida, C. (2010) 'Income support policy in Canada and the UK: Different, but much the same,' *Disability & Society* 25(6), 673–686. <http://dx.doi.org/10.1080/09687599.2010.505739> [accessed 10 March 2022].

Marks, D. (1999) 'Dimensions of oppression: Theorising the embodied subject,' *Disability & Society* 14(5), 611–626.

Marx, K. (1867) *Capital: A Critique of Political Economy. Volume I. Book one: the Process of Production of Capital.* Marxist Archives. <https://www.marxists.org/archive/marx/works/1867-c1/> [accessed 10 March 2022].>

Mays, J. M. (2006) 'Feminist disability theory: Domestic violence against women with a disability,' *Disability & Society* 21(2), 147–158. <https://doi.org/10.1080/09687590500498077> [accessed 10 March 2022].

McCall, L. (2005). The Complexity of Intersectionality. *Signs: Journal of Women in Culture and Society* 30(3), 1771-1800.

McCallum, R. (2010) United Nations Convention on the Rights of Persons with Disabilities: some reflections. *Legal Studies Research Paper, 10*(30). University of Sydney Law School.

McIvor, S. D. (2004) 'Aboriginal women unmasked: Using equality litigation to advance women's rights,' *Canadian Journal of Women and the Law/Revue femrnes et droit* 16(1), 106–136.

Meekosha, H. (2002), 'Virtual activists? Women and the making of identities of disability,' *Hypatia* 17(3), 67–88.

Meekosha, H. & Shuttleworth, R. (2009) 'What's so "critical" about critical disability studies?' *Australian Journal of Human Rights* 15(1), 47–75.

Menzies R. & Palys, T. (2006) 'Turbulent spirits: Aboriginal patients in the British Columbia psychiatric system, 1879–1950' in J.E. Moran & D. Wright (eds), *Mental health and Canadian society: Historical perspectives* (pp. 69–96). McGill–Queen's University Press.

Meyers, D. T. (2002) *Gender in the Mirror: Cultural Imagery and Women's Agency.* Oxford University Press.

Million, D. (2013) *Therapeutic Nations: Healing in an age of Indigenous Human Rights.* The University of Arizona Press.

Mitchinson, W. (1987) 'Gender and insanity as characteristics of the insane: a nineteenth-century case,' *Canadian Bulletin of Medical History/Bulletin Canadien d'histoire de la Médecine* 4(2), 99–117.

Morris, J. (1993) 'Feminism and disability,' *Feminist Review 43*, 57–70. <http://doi.org.ezproxy.library.yorku.ca/10.2307/1395069>.

Morris, J. (1991) *Pride against prejudice: transforming attitudes to disability.* New Society.

Morrison, A., Ellsberg, M. and Bott, S. (2007) 'Addressing Gender-Based Violence: A Critical Review of Interventions,' *The World Bank Research Observer* 22(1), 25–51.

Muthukrishna, N., Sokoya, G. and Moodley, S. (2009) 'Gender and disability: An intersectional analysis of experiences of ten disabled women in Kwazu-Natal,' *Gender & Behavior* 7(1), 2264–2282.

National Resource Center on Domestic Violence. (2015) *Violence Against Trans and Non-binary People.* VAWNet. <https://vawnet.org/sc/serving-trans-and-non-binary-survivors-domestic-and-sexual-violence/violence-against-trans-and> [accessed 10 March 2022].

Nelson, J. (2011) 'Invisible no longer: Images of disability in the media', in P. Lester & S.D. Ross (eds) *Images that injure: Pictorial stereotypes in the media* (3rd edn) (pp. 274–291). ABC CILO, LLC.

Nixon, J. (2009) 'Domestic violence and women with disabilities: locating the issue on the periphery of social movements,' *Disability & Society* 24(1), 77–89.

Odette, F. (2013) 'Violence against women with disabilities and Deaf women,' *The Learning Network.* Issue 7.

Oliver, M. (1997) 'Emancipatory research: Realistic goal or impossible dream?', in C. Barnes and G. Mercer (eds), *Doing Disability Research* (pp. 15–31). The Disability Press.

Oliver, M. (1990) *The politics of disablement: a sociological approach.* St. Martin's Press.

Olsvik, V. (2006) 'Vulnerable, exposed and invisible: A study of violence and abuse against women with physical disabilities,' *Scandinavian Journal of*

*Disability* 8(2–3), 85–98. <http://dx.doi.org/10.1080/15017410600731343> [accessed 10 March 2022].

Ontario Human Rights Commission. (2016) *Policy on Ableism and Discrimination based on Disability.* <http://www.ohrc.on.ca/en/policy-ableism-and-discrimi-nation-based-disability> [accessed 10 March 2022].

Ontario Human Rights Commission. (2014) *Human Rights in Ontario: Gender identity and Gender Expression.* <http://www.ohrc.on.ca/en/gender-identity-and-gender-expression-brochure> [accessed 10 March 2022].

Ontario Human Rights Commission. (2001) *An Intersectional Approach to Discrimination: Addressing Multiple Grounds in Human Rights Claims.* Discussion Paper. <http://www.ohrc.on.ca/en/intersectional-approach-discrimination-addressing-multiple-grounds-human-rights-claims> [accessed 10 March 2022].

Peate, I. (2019) 'Gender-based violence,' *British Journal of Nursing* 28(10), 607. <https://www.magonlinelibrary.com/doi/abs/10.12968/bjon.2019.28.10.607>.

Price, J. (2011) 'The seeds of a movement – disabled women and their struggle to organize', in S. Batliwala (ed.). *Changing Their World* (2nd edn). Association of Women's Rights in Development. <https://www.awid.org/sites/default/files/atoms/files/changing_their_world_2_-_disabled_women_and_their_struggle_to_organize.pdf> [accessed 10 March 2022].

Putnam, M. (2005) 'Conceptualizing disability', *Journal of Disability Policy Studies* 16(3), 188–198. <https://doi.org/10.1177/10442073050160030601> [accessed 10 March 2022].

Quinn, G. (2011) *Disability and Human Rights: a New Field in the United Nations.* (Presentation handout). Summer School on the Convention on the Rights of Persons with Disabilities.

Renwick, R., Yoshida, K., Eacrett, E. and Rose, N. (2018) 'Meaning of staring and the starer–staree relationship related to men living with acquired spinal cord injuries', *American Journal of Men's Health 12*(2), 283–291. <https://doi.org/10.1177/1557988316632297> [accessed 10 March 2022].

Rioux, M.H., Crawford, C., Ticoll, M. & Bach, M. (1997) 'Uncovering the shape of violence: A research methodology rooted in the experience of people with disabilities', in C. Barnes and G. Mercer (Eds), *Doing disability research* (pp. 190–207). The Disability Press.

Rioux, M. & Patton, L. (2004) 'Employment equity and disability: moving forward to achieve employment integration and fulfil promises of inclusion and participation', In C. Agócs (Ed.). *Employment equity in Canada: The legacy of the Abella report* (pp. 133–155). University of Toronto Press.

Robinson, M. (2006) *A Voice for Human Rights.* University of Pennsylvania Press.

Rodríguez-Roldán, V. M. (2020). 'The intersection between disability and LGBT discrimination and marginalization', *American University Journal of Gender, Social Policy & the Law, 28*(3), 429–439. Available at: <https://digitalcommons.wcl.american.edu/jgspl/vol28/iss3/2>

Roeher Institute. (1995) *Harm's Way: The Many Faces of Violence and Abuse against Persons with Disabilities.* Roeher Institute.

Roman, L. G., Brown, S., Noble, S., Wainer, R. and Young, A. E. (2009) 'No time for nostalgia!: asylum-making, medicalized colonialism in British Columbia (1859–97) and artistic praxis for social transformation', *International Journal of Qualitative Studies in Education* 22(1), 17–63.

Schwartz, D., Blue, E., McDonald, M., Giuliani, G., Weber, G., Seirup, H., Rose, S., Elkis-Albuhoff, D., Rosenfeld, J., Perkins, A. (2010) 'Dispelling stereotypes: Promoting disability equality through film', *Disability & Society* 25(7), 841–848. <https://doi.org/10.1080/09687599.2010.520898> [accessed 10 March 2022].

Seifert, H. and Goldstein, J. (2016) *A Case for Financial Inclusion of Persons with Disabilities: CBM Livelihood Technical Guide.* CBM and the Centre for Financial Inclusion at Accion. <https://www.cbm.org/fileadmin/user_upload/Publications/Case_for_Financial_Inclusion_-final-_May_2016.docx>.

Serano, J. (2013). *Excluded: making feminist and queer movements more inclusive.*

Serano, J. (2007). *Whipping Girl: A transsexual woman on sexism and the scapegoating of femininity.* Berkeley: Seal Press.

Shakespeare, T. (2006) *Disability Rights and Wrongs.* Routledge.

de Silva de Alwis, R. (2009). Mining the Intersections: Advancing the Rights of Women and Children with Disabilities within an Interrelated web of Human Rights. Faculty Scholarship at Penn Law. 1697. <https://scholarship.law.upenn.edu/faculty_scholarship/1697> [accessed 10 March 2022].

Sinek, S. (2009) *How Great Leaders Inspire Action.* TED. Ideas worth Spreading. <https://www.ted.com/talks/simon_sinek_how_great_leaders_inspire_action?language=en#t-263134> [accessed 10 March 2022].

Singal, N. (2010) 'Doing disability research in a southern context', *Disability & Society* 25(4), 415–426.

Slater, J. and Liddiard, K. (2018) 'Why disability studies scholars must challenge transmisogyny and transphobia', *Canadian Journal of Disability Studies* 7(2). p. 83–93.

Smith, A. (2005) *Conquest: Sexual Violence and American Indian Genocide.* South End Press.

Status of Women Canada. (2018) *About Gender-based Violence.* Government of Canada. <https://cfc-swc.gc.ca/violence/knowledge-connaissance/fs-fi-1-en.html>.

Stein, M. (2007) 'Disability human rights', *California Law Review* 95(1), 75–122.

Stemler, S. (2001) 'An overview of content analysis' *Practical Assessment, Research & Evaluation* 7(17). <http://PAREonline.net/getvn.asp?v=7&n=17> [accessed 10 March 2022].

Stone, E. and Priestley, M. (1996) 'Parasites, pawns and partners: disability research and the role of non-disabled researchers', *British Journal of Sociology,* 47(4), 699–716.

Strauss, A. and Corbin, J. (1994) 'Grounded theory methodology', In N.K. Denzin & Y.S. Lincoln (Eds.), *Handbook of qualitative research* (pp. 217–285). SAGE Publications Ltd.

Sullivan, J. R. (2012) 'Skype: An appropriate method of data collection for qualitative interviews?', *The Hilltop Review* 6(1), 53–60.

Titchkosky, T. (2005) 'Disability in the news: a reconsideration of reading', *Disability and Society* 20(6,) 655–668. <http://doi.org/10.1080/09687590500249082> [accessed 10 March 2022].

Tuan, Y. F. (1977). *Space and place: The perspective of experience.* Minneapolis: University of Minnesota.

United Nations. (2013) *Study on the Situation of Indigenous Persons with Disabilities, with a Particular Focus on Challenges faced with Regard to the full Enjoyment of Human Rights and Inclusion in Development.* Permanent Forum on Indigenous Issues. 12th Session.

United Nations. (2007) *From Exclusion to Equality – Realising rights of Persons with Disabilities: Handbook for Parliamentarians on the Convention on the Rights of Persons with Disabilities and its Optional Protocol.* Geneva, Switzerland; SRO-Kundig.

United Nations. (2006) *Convention on the Rights of Persons with Disabilities and Optional Protocol.* <http://www.un.org/disabilities/documents/convention/convoptprot-e.pdf> [accessed 10 March 2022].

United Nations Population Fund. (2018a) *Women and Young Persons with Disabilities: Guidelines for Providing Rights-based and Gender-responsive Services to Address Gender-based Violence and Sexual and Reproductive Health and Rights.* United Nations Population Fund & Women Enabled International. <https://www.unfpa.org/featured-publication/women-and-young-persons-disabilities> [accessed 10 March 2022].

United Nations Population Fund. (2018b) *Young Persons with Disabilities: Global Study on Ending Gender-based Violence, and Realizing Sexual and Reproductive Health and Rights.* <https://www.unfpa.org/sites/default/files/pub-pdf/Final_Global_Study_English_3_Oct.pdf> [accessed 10 March 2022].

Vecova Centre for Disability Services and Research. (2011) *Violence Against Women with Disabilities: Violence Prevention Review.* Canadian Women's Foundation.

Vehmas, S. and Watson, N. (2014) 'Moral wrongs, disadvantages, and disability: A critique of critical disability studies', *Disability & Society* 29(4), 638–650.

Vernon, A. (1997) 'Reflexivity: The dilemmas of researching from the inside', in C. Barnes and G. Mercer (eds), *Doing disability research.* (pp. 158–176). The Disability Press.

Vernon, A. (1996a) 'A Stranger in Many Camps: The experience of Disabled Black and Ethnic Minority Women', in J. Morris, ed. Encounters With strangers: Feminism and Disability. London: Women's Press.

Walliman, N. (2006) *SAGE Course Companions: Social Research Methods.* SAGE Publications Ltd.

Weber, R. P. (1990) *Basic Content Analysis* (2nd ed.). Sage Publications.

Weldon, S. L. (2006) 'Inclusion, solidarity, and social movements: The global movement against gender violence', *Perspectives on Politics* 4(1), 55–74. <https://doi.org/10.1017/S1537592706060063> [accessed 10 March 2022].

Williams, T. K. (2012) *Understanding Internalized Oppression: a theoretical Conceptualization of Internalized Subordination. Dissertations.* Paper 627.

Withers, A. J. (2013). *Disabling Trans: Politics Implications and Possibilities of Constructions of Trans as a Disability.* <https://stillmyrevolution.files.wordpress.com/2015/05/withers-fully-completed-mrp-doccument.pdf> [accessed 27 March 2022]

Women Enabled International (2020) *COVID-19 at the Intersection of Gender and Disability: Findings of a Global Human Rights survey, March to April 2020.* <https://www.empowerwomen.org/en/resources/documents/2020/08/covid-19-at-the-intersection-of-gender-and-disability-findings-of-a-global-human-rights-survey?lang=en>

World Health Organization (WHO) (2019) *Coronavirus disease (COVID-19).* <https://www.who.int/health-topics/coronavirus#tab=tab_1> [accessed 10 March 2022].

World Health Organization, & World Bank. (2011) *World Report of Disability.* World Health Organization.

Young, I. M. (1990) 'Five Faces of Oppression', In I.M Young (ed), *Justice and the politics of difference* (pp. 39–65). Princeton University Press.

Zhang, L. & Haller B. (2013) 'Consuming image: How mass media impact the identity of people with disabilities', *Communication Quarterly* 61(3), 319–334. <https://doi.org/10.1080/01463373.2013.776988> [accessed 10 March 2022].

# Index

www.ingramcontent.com/pod-product-compliance
Lightning Source LLC
Chambersburg PA
CBHW062108040426
42336CB00042B/2666